DOUGHNUTS!

100 DOUGH–LICIOUS RECIPES

CAROL BECKERMAN
DAWN OTWELL

DOUGHNUTS!

100 DOUGH–LICIOUS RECIPES

BARRON'S

A QUINTET BOOK

First edition for the United States
and Canada published in 2014 by
Barron's Educational Series, Inc.

All inquiries should be addressed to:
Barron's Educational Series, Inc.
250 Wireless Boulevard
Hauppauge, NY 11788
www.barronseduc.com

Library of Congress Control Number: 2014938657
ISBN: 978-1-4380-0463-1
QTT.DNUT

Conceived, designed, and produced by:
Quintet Publishing
4th Floor, Sheridan House
114-116 Western Road
Hove BN3 1DD
UK

Project Editor: Caroline Elliker
Designer: Astwood Designs
Photographers: Tony Briscoe, Claire Winfield
Food Stylists: Lucy Heeley, Vicki Smallwood
Art Director: Michael Charles
Editorial Director: Emma Bastow
Publisher: Mark Searle

Manufactured in China by 1010 Printing International Ltd.

9 8 7 6 5 4 3 2 1

CONTENTS

INTRODUCTION

DOUGHNUTS ARE DELICIOUS

Doughnuts are a childish pleasure you never grow out of. From European festival food to everyday American breakfasts, our favorite treat has taken on many forms throughout its history. Whether it is sticky and filled with preserves, or airy, cream-filled, and glazed with chocolate, each one is completely, thoroughly, compulsively, satisfyingly delicious.

Doughnuts come in all shapes and sizes. They are the perfect way to treat yourself, friends, or family on a lazy weekend, or to indulge in a baking adventure. Store-bought doughnuts are great, but homemade ones are definitely better.

The word "doughnut" has become an umbrella that includes crullers, fritters, yum-yums, twists, rings, and round cakes; those filled with preserves or cream, with holes and without, and even the holes themselves. They should be warm enough to take away the fall chill, and sweet enough so that you cannot stop at one—crusty on the outside and soft and tender on the inside. Served with steaming hot coffee or creamy hot chocolate, nothing beats the squish of the first bite into a soft and fluffy, freshly-made and glazed doughnut.

The doughnut chains have reigned supreme in the doughnut world for the past few decades, but as boutique bakeries spring up here and there, doughnuts' popularity continues to grow. Unique doughnuts with interesting and innovative flavors are cropping up in major cities across the world. Maple and bacon doughnuts, doughnut sandwiches, and interesting inventions using meringue or peanut butter cups show that doughnuts are not just for dunking anymore.

MAKING DOUGHNUTS

There are three basic types of doughnut. These are yeast-raised, cake, and cruller. A doughnut that uses yeast for leavening produces a light and airy doughnut. They often have stretchy rather than crumbly interiors and generally feel lighter in your hand. Cake doughnuts are made from a cakelike batter, which is leavened with baking powder or soda. The texture is different from a yeast doughnut, as it can be either denser or more crumbly. The third type, a cruller, is a twisted fried doughnut, either in a ring shape or in a long straight strip. This type of doughnut is made from choux pastry, the same dough that is used to make profiteroles.

Yeast-raised doughnuts and cake doughnuts can be deep-fried or baked, and crullers are always deep-fried.

Although easier to make than generally thought, more steps are involved in producing yeast-raised doughnuts, so they usually take longer than cake doughnuts. When making dough for yeast-raised doughnuts, many factors can affect the consistency of the dough. Altitude, humidity, temperature, and type of flour can all change the amount of liquid needed at the time. The dough should be quite sticky, but not overly so. If it seems too dry, add a little more liquid, and if it seems too sticky, add a little more flour. You will soon start to get a feel for the dough, and will be able to produce light and airy doughnuts from a few basic ingredients.

USING YEAST

Yeast is not scary. It is a living organism that, as it grows, converts its food (either sugar or starch) into alcohol and carbon dioxide through the process of fermentation. In this book we call for two types of yeast—active dry yeast and instant (also sold as fast-acting or rapid rise) yeast.

Active dry yeast usually needs to be dissolved in liquid and set aside for a period of time for fermentation to

start. This is called proofing. To speed this process up, and to check that the yeast is indeed active, you can add a teaspoon of sugar to the warm liquid with the yeast. The temperature of the liquid is very important. This is because if the liquid is too cold, it will fail to wake up the yeast, and if it is too hot, the heat will kill the yeast. The optimum temperature is 110°F (43°C), which is just warm, not hot. Use a thermometer to check it, if you want.

Both active dry and instant yeast are baker's yeast dried into granules; instant yeast granules are finer than active dry. This means that instant yeast can be mixed straight into the flour; it does not need to be dissolved in liquid first. However, salt will stop instant yeast from fermenting, so keep them apart on separate sides of the mixing bowl. Use whichever type of yeast is called for in the recipe.

MIXING AND KNEADING THE DOUGH

Following the recipe, combine the ingredients in either a large bowl or the bowl of a stand mixer. If you're mixing by hand, you can mix the ingredients together with the (clean) fingers of one hand, stirring the flour and liquid around and gradually incorporating the flour from the sides of the bowl.

Keep mixing until all the flour has been incorporated. This is quite messy as the mixture will stick to your hands, but it will become smoother as the dough begins to form. If you are using a stand mixer, combine the ingredients using the dough hook attachment.

Now you will begin kneading, an important part of making dough, because it develops the gluten in the flour to make a good texture for the doughnuts. If using a mixer, knead for about 4 minutes with the dough hook attachment. If you are kneading by hand, either turn the dough out onto a lightly floured work surface or knead it in the bowl.

As the dough will be quite sticky, especially to begin with, you may find it easier to use the bowl. Just keep folding the dough into the middle, and turning it around as you do so, finding a procedure that suits you. Repeat this action for about 5 minutes (less time than for making bread). If you use a work surface, knead using your knuckles and hands, punching into the dough and turning it around as you do so. Whether you're kneading by hand or with your mixer, try not to add too much extra flour at this stage, as that would change the texture of the finished doughnut.

Cover the bowl with plastic wrap, or transfer to a lightly oiled bowl, turn the dough to coat it all over, cover, and leave until doubled in size. If you place the bowl somewhere warm, such as in front of a radiator or in your oven with the door open slightly (if you can put it on a really low heat), this will take approximately an hour. Leaving the bowl at room temperature will slightly slow down the rise, and leaving it in the refrigerator will slow down the rise considerably.

When you are proofing your doughnuts for the second time, after rolling and cutting them out, they should be covered to prevent a skin from forming. Use plastic wrap that has been lightly sprayed with nonstick spray oil.

This stops the dough sticking to the plastic wrap, which would inhibit the rise and give a tough doughnut. Leave the doughnuts somewhere warm again. If you forget the doughnuts, and find they have over-proofed, as an emergency rescue, you can knead them again, cut them out and proof once more, although this will give you fewer doughnuts.

BAKING DOUGHNUTS

If the doughnuts are made using dough, they should be rolled and cut out using a doughnut cutter or a biscuit cutter (with no hole in the center). If you are using cookie sheets, they should be either lined with parchment paper or sprayed with nonstick spray oil to prevent sticking. Oven-baked doughnuts made with batter can either be made in a 6- or 12-cup doughnut pan, which should be sprayed with nonstick spray oil to prevent the doughnuts from sticking. When filling the doughnut pans, try to get the same amount of batter in each cup.

This is much easier if you use a pastry bag. If you can find them, disposable pastry bags are an excellent invention. Snip off the end to make it the correct size for filling your pans, then turn the tip over and secure it with a paper clip to prevent the mixture oozing out before you are ready. Stand the pastry bag in a large glass to keep it in place to fill it with mixture. Remove the paper clip and proceed to fill the pans.

DEEP-FRYING DOUGHNUTS

To deep-fry your doughnuts, there are no hard and fast rules for which fat gives the best results. Canola oil is heart-friendly, and many people like the taste of sunflower oil. Some traditionalists like to use a fat that is hard when cold, but all give good results, so use your favorite.

For deep-frying, you will need either a deep-fat fryer or a large heavy-bottomed pan. You will need enough vegetable oil in your chosen pan to come about halfway up the side. If you fill your pan too much, it can overflow, which could be dangerous.

Too little oil means the doughnuts will not deep-fry. To deep-fry doughnuts in oil, the most important factor is the temperature of the oil. Use a deep-frying thermometer to monitor the temperature, and keep the oil as close to 360°F (182°C) as possible.

Do not overcrowd the pan, as this lowers the temperature of the oil too much and affects the length of time needed to cook the doughnuts through to the middle.

As a general rule, the following timings work well for an oven heated at 360°F (182°C):

Doughnut holes:	**1 minute first side,**
	½ minute second side
Mini doughnuts:	**1 minute each side**
Doughnut rounds	
3 ½-inch (8.75cm):	**3 minutes first side,**
	2 minutes second side
Doughnut rings	
3 ½-inch (8.75cm):	**2 minutes each side**

When placing the doughnuts in the oil, slide a thin palette knife under each one and lower it into the oil very carefully, trying not to damage the doughnut's surface. Never leave them unattended while they are cooking.

When you flip the doughnuts over in the pan, watch that they do not brown too much. If they do, turn the heat down a little. When cooked, remove them with a wire spoon or spider, and place them on a double layer of paper towels either on the work surface or on cookie sheets.

When you first start making doughnuts, it is a good idea to test one. Cook as directed and when cool enough to handle, cut into the middle and check that it is cooked through. Press down with your fingers and check that it springs back nicely.

FROSTING AND GLAZING

You will learn very quickly about the correct consistency of the glaze for coating the doughnuts. It needs to be thick enough to coat well, and not too runny, or it will all drip off. Humidity and temperature can affect the consistency of the glaze. Follow the recipes, but use your judgment, and add the liquid a little at a time if you can—until it looks and feels right. It also helps to sift powdered sugar before using, to prevent lumps.

Melting chocolate is best done in a bowl over barely simmering water. The water should not touch the bottom of the bowl. For drizzling melted chocolate over the doughnuts to decorate them, disposable pastry bags work well. Cut the end off to give a very small opening, then fold the tip over and secure it with a paper clip. This stops the chocolate running out before you are ready. Leave the melted chocolate for a short time until it is cool enough to handle, stand the pastry bag in a tall glass, and pour in the chocolate. Remove the paper clip and decorate.

To dip doughnuts in glaze or melted chocolate, pick up the cooled doughnut with your fingers and carefully dip the top half in the glaze. Twist the doughnut slightly to make sure all the surface is covered, and lift the doughnut. Hold it above the bowl at a slight angle, and wait while the excess glaze drips off. Set on a wire rack or paper towels.

SERVING DOUGHNUTS

If possible, serve your doughnuts immediately, the day they are made. This is when they are at their optimum freshness. If this is not possible, or if you have one or two left over, you can store them in an airtight container for a short period of time only. If you still have one or two remaining, Truffle Cake Balls (page 83) that uses stale doughnuts formed into balls and dipped in chocolate.

EQUIPMENT

Not all the recipes will require all the equipment listed below, but it will help you enormously if you have these on hand.

- **Stand mixer (optional, but great if you have one)**
- **Large and small mixing bowls**
- **Large cookie sheets**
- **Parchment paper for lining pans**
- **Measuring cups**
- **Rolling pin**
- **Doughnut pans, 6-cup and 12-cup**
- **Palette knife**
- **Slotted spoon or spider**
- **Plastic wrap**
- **Heavy, large pan for deep-frying**
- **Thermometer for monitoring oil temperature when deep-frying**
- **Paper towels for draining**
- **Small pans for making frosting**
- **Wire racks for cooling and draining**
- **Pastry bags and tips**

Chapter 1

MINIS & HOLES

Little morsels of sticky sweetness are just right for small children with little fingers, and great to add to a buffet or brunch menu. Making a selection provides something for everyone, or an excuse to sample lots of different tastes and treats.

BUTTERSCOTCH HOLES WITH MAPLE SYRUP

These little doughnut holes are quick to make and delicious to eat, with a sweet maple syrup taste and a rich butterscotch glaze, drizzled with dark chocolate.

INGREDIENTS

For the doughnuts
- 2 cups (250g) all-purpose flour
- ½ cup (100g) brown sugar
- 3 teaspoons baking powder
- ½ teaspoon salt
- 1 ½ teaspoons ground cinnamon
- 4 tablespoons canola oil
- ⅔ cup (160ml) whole milk
- 2 tablespoons maple syrup
- 1 large egg, room temperature
- Vegetable oil for deep-frying

For the glaze
- ¼ cup (60ml) whole milk
- 1 ⅓ cups (130g) powdered sugar, sifted
- ¼ cup (80g) butterscotch chips

For the decoration
- ¼ cup (80g) semisweet chocolate chips, melted

METHOD

In a medium bowl, whisk together the flour, brown sugar, baking powder, salt, and cinnamon.

In a small bowl, whisk the canola oil, milk, maple syrup, and egg together. Pour into the flour mixture and mix until just combined.

Heat the oil in a large, heavy pan to 360°F (182°C). Drop teaspoons of the dough into the hot oil in batches, and cook for 1 minute on the first side, ½ minute on the second, until golden brown. Drain on paper towels.

Make the glaze. Heat the milk in a small pan over a medium heat, until just below a simmer, and add the powdered sugar a tablespoon at a time until it is all incorporated. Add the butterscotch chips and keep heating and stirring until melted and the glaze is smooth. Keep warm over a low heat, stirring occasionally to keep it runny. Add a little more milk if the glaze becomes too thick.

Dip one side of the doughnut holes, one at a time, in the glaze and transfer to a wire rack to drain. Drizzle each one with melted semisweet chocolate chips (use a pastry bag or a plastic bag with the corner cut off). Let set before serving.

Makes about 36

DOUGHNUT PASTRY HOLES

*Because these little doughnut holes are made with croissant pastry, they puff up
beautifully during cooking. Serve warm, dredged with sugar and cinnamon.*

INGREDIENTS

For the pastry holes
- ⅓ cup (80ml) whole milk, warmed
- 1 teaspoon superfine sugar
- 1 package (2 ¼ teaspoons) active dry yeast
- 1 ⅓ cups (170g) white bread flour
- 2 tablespoons superfine sugar
- 1 large egg, room temperature, lightly beaten
- 1 tablespoon unsalted butter, softened
- 1 cup (125g) all-purpose flour
- 1 teaspoon salt
- ½ cup (115g) unsalted butter, very cold,
  in small cubes
- Vegetable oil for deep-frying

For the decoration
- 1 ½ cups (300g) superfine sugar
- 1–2 teaspoons ground cinnamon (to taste)

METHOD

Line a large cookie sheet with parchment paper.

Place warm milk in a large bowl, stir in 1 teaspoon superfine sugar, sprinkle
with yeast, and leave for 10–15 minutes until frothy. Add ⅓ cup (40g) white
bread flour and beat well. Add 2 tablespoons superfine sugar and the egg, and
beat smooth. Add 1 tablespoon softened butter, beat, and set aside. Put 1 cup
(125g) all-purpose flour, remaining bread flour, and salt into the bowl of a
food processor. Add cold butter cubes and pulse briefly until butter is the size
of peas. Transfer to a bowl, cover, and refrigerate for 2 hours.

Turn chilled dough out onto a lightly floured surface, knead lightly, and roll
into a 15 x 5-inch (40 x 12cm) rectangle. Working quickly, fold the dough into
thirds, bringing the bottom third up and folding the top third down. Put into
a greased plastic bag and chill for 1 hour. Repeat rolling and chilling twice
more. You can leave the dough in the refrigerator overnight at this stage.

Roll out dough to 1 ½ inches (3.75cm) thick, and cut with a ½-inch (1.25cm)
cutter into about 24 pieces. Reroll the dough as necessary. Set the pieces an
inch (2.5cm) apart on the cookie sheet, and cover loosely with plastic wrap
that has been sprayed with oil. Chill for about 1 hour.

Heat the oil in a heavy, large pan to 360°F (182°C). Fry the pastry holes
until golden brown, about 3 minutes in total, flipping them over every
minute or so. Drain on paper towels. Mix the sugar and cinnamon and roll
the holes around to coat all over. Transfer to a wire rack until ready to serve.
Serve warm.

Makes about 24

TIP

There are many ways you could serve these little pastry holes. Choose
any of the many frostings and glazes throughout the book. Or fill with
whipped cream like profiteroles and serve with chocolate sauce and ice
cream layered in a tall glass, with a swirl of cream and a cherry on the top.

S'MORES MINIS

These mini doughnuts are baked in the oven and smothered in marshmallow frosting before being sprinkled with graham cracker crumbs and drizzled with chocolate.

INGREDIENTS

For the doughnuts
- ½ cup (60g) all-purpose flour
- ¼ cup (50g) superfine sugar
- 2 tablespoons unsweetened cocoa powder, sifted
- ¼ teaspoon baking powder
- ¼ teaspoon baking soda
- ¼ teaspoon salt
- 3 tablespoons Greek yogurt
- 1 ½ tablespoons whole milk
- 1 large egg, room temperature
- 2 tablespoons canola oil
- 1 teaspoon vanilla extract

For the frosting
- 3 tablespoons (45g) unsalted butter
- ¼ cup (60ml) water
- 1 teaspoon vanilla extract
- 2 cups (150g) white mini marshmallows
- 2 cups (200g) powdered sugar, sifted
- ¼ teaspoon salt

For the decoration
- 3 tablespoons graham cracker crumbs
- ¼ cup (80g) semisweet chocolate chips, melted

METHOD

Spray a 12-cup mini-doughnut pan with oil. Preheat the oven to 350°F (175°C).

In a large bowl, whisk together the flour, sugar, cocoa powder, baking powder, baking soda, and salt.

In a separate bowl, whisk together the yogurt, milk, egg, canola oil, and vanilla extract. Pour into the flour mixture and stir to combine. Using a pastry bag (a disposable one is great for this, or use a plastic bag with the corner cut off), fill the doughnut cups two-thirds full. Bake in the oven for about 10 minutes, or until a toothpick inserted in the center comes out clean. Let cool in the pan for 5 minutes, then carefully transfer the doughnuts to a wire rack to cool.

Make the frosting. In a small pan, over medium heat, melt the butter, water, and vanilla, stirring occasionally. Add the marshmallows and stir until they have melted and the mixture is smooth. In a medium bowl, whisk the powdered sugar and salt, and pour the melted marshmallows over, whisking until combined. Dip half of each doughnut into the frosting and place back on the rack to drain. Sprinkle each one with graham cracker crumbs and drizzle with melted semisweet chocolate.

Makes 12

CHOCOLATE AND CARAMEL HOLES

These gorgeous little doughnuts are raised with yeast and filled with caramel and chocolate, before being deep-fried and rolled in sugar.

INGREDIENTS

For the doughnuts
- ⅔ cup (160ml) whole milk, warmed
- 1 teaspoon superfine sugar
- 1 package (2 ¼ teaspoons) active dry yeast
- 3 ½ cups (440g) all-purpose flour
- ⅔ cup (130g) superfine sugar
- 2 teaspoons salt
- 2 large eggs, room temperature, lightly beaten
- ½ cup (115g) salted butter, room temperature, cut into small pieces
- 25 store-bought soft caramels
- 25 small squares milk chocolate
- Vegetable oil for deep-frying

For the decoration
- 1 cup (200g) superfine sugar

METHOD

Line two large cookie sheets with parchment paper.

Pour the warm milk into a medium bowl, stir in the teaspoon of superfine sugar, sprinkle with the yeast, and set aside for 10–15 minutes until frothy.

In the bowl of a stand mixer fitted with a dough hook, stir the flour, ⅔ cup (130g) superfine sugar, and salt. Add the yeast mixture and beaten eggs, and mix until the dough comes together. With the mixer on medium speed, add a piece of butter, fully incorporating before adding the next piece. This should take about 5–7 minutes. The dough will be sticky, but not very. If it seems too wet, add a little flour; if it feels too dry, add a little water. Put the dough in a lightly oiled bowl, turn it around to coat it all over, and cover with plastic wrap. Leave in a warm place for an hour or so, or until doubled.

Turn the dough out onto a lightly floured work surface and punch down. Knead a couple of times. Break off 22 equal-sized pieces of dough (I like to weigh each piece to ensure they are the same size, 1 ½ ounces/45g). Place a caramel and a square of chocolate in the middle of each. Wrap the dough around the filling and pinch dough together well. Set on the cookie sheets, about an inch (2.5cm) apart, with the seam underneath, cover with plastic wrap sprayed with oil, and let rest for an hour.

Heat the oil in a large, heavy pan to 360°F (182°C). Fry the doughnuts for 2 minutes per side until golden brown. Drain on paper towels. When cool enough to handle, roll in the sugar until coated all over.

Makes about 22

MINI CARAMEL PECAN MONKEY BREAD

*These sweet little buns, glossy with glaze, are wonderful for breakfast
or an ideal treat for weekends.*

INGREDIENTS

For the doughnuts
- ½ cup (120ml) warm water
- 1 teaspoon superfine sugar
- 1 package (2 ¼ teaspoons) active
  dry yeast
- 1 ½ cups (190g) white bread flour
- 1 ½ cups (190g) whole wheat bread flour
- ⅔ cup (130g) superfine sugar
- 2 teaspoons ground cinnamon
- 1 teaspoon salt
- ½ cup (120ml) whole milk, warmed
- ⅔ cup (160ml) vegetable oil
- 1 cup (125g) toasted pecan halves

For the coating
- ¼ cup (50g) superfine sugar mixed with
  2 teaspoons ground cinnamon

For the topping
- ¼ cup (60g) salted butter
- ½ cup (100g) brown sugar
- 1 tablespoon maple syrup
- 2 teaspoon vanilla extract
- ½ teaspoon salt

METHOD

Place the warm water in a bowl, stir in the teaspoon of superfine sugar, sprinkle with yeast, and set aside for 10–15 minutes until frothy.

With a stand mixer fitted with a dough hook, mix together the flours, sugar, cinnamon, and salt. Make a well in the center and pour in the yeast liquid, warm milk, and vegetable oil. Mix on medium until a dough comes together. Knead for 5–7 minutes, until the dough is soft, smooth, and elastic. If it is too sticky, add a little more flour; too dry, add a little more water. Transfer to a large oiled bowl, turn the dough around, cover with plastic wrap, and leave for an hour or so until doubled.

Turn dough out onto a lightly floured work surface, and punch down. Divide the dough into 16 pieces, and cut each piece into quarters. Spray two 12-cup muffin pans with oil and place 4 or 5 toasted pecan halves into each cup.

Roll each dough piece in the cinnamon sugar coating and place 4 in each cup.

Heat the topping ingredients gently, stirring continuously, until dissolved. Spoon 1–2 teaspoons over the top of the doughnuts in each muffin cup. Cover with oiled plastic wrap and leave for an hour.

Preheat the oven to 350°F (175°C). Bake for 20–25 minutes. Let cool in the pans for 5 minutes before inverting onto a wire rack to cool. Serve warm.

Makes 16

LITTLE PEANUT BUTTER DOUGHNUT HOLES WITH CHOCOLATE FROSTING

These little doughnut holes are just-the-right-size peanut butter and chocolate-dipped treats.

INGREDIENTS

For the doughnuts
- ¼ cup (65g) smooth peanut butter
- ¼ cup (50g) superfine sugar
- ⅓ cup (80ml) plus 1 tablespoon whole milk
- 1 tablespoon vegetable oil
- 1 large egg, room temperature, lightly beaten
- 1 teaspoon vanilla extract
- 1 cup (125g) all-purpose flour
- 1 teaspoon baking powder
- ½ teaspoon salt
- ½ teaspoon ground cinnamon

For the frosting
- ¼ cup (60g) unsalted butter
- 2 tablespoons whole milk
- 1 tablespoon half-and-half
- 1 teaspoon light corn syrup
- 1 teaspoon vanilla extract
- ⅓ cup (100g) semisweet chocolate chips

For the decoration
- 3 tablespoons chopped pecans

METHOD

Preheat the oven to 325°F (160°C) and spray two 12-cup mini-muffin pans with oil.

Using an electric mixer, whisk together the peanut butter and superfine sugar until fluffy. Add milk, oil, egg, and vanilla, and continue to mix until combined. Add the flour, baking powder, salt, and cinnamon, and mix until smooth. Spoon the batter into the muffin cups, filling them three-quarters full. Bake in the preheated oven for 8–10 minutes, or until a toothpick inserted into the center comes out clean. Cool in the pans for 5 minutes before turning out onto a wire rack to cool.

Make the frosting. In a small pan, melt the butter with the milk, half-and-half, corn syrup, and vanilla extract. Add the chocolate chips and stir until melted and smooth. Dip the top of the doughnuts into the frosting and place back on the wire rack to cool. When the frosting is almost set, sprinkle the tops with chopped pecans.

Makes 18

SUGARED LEMON CURD-FILLED DOUGHNUT HOLES

These little morsels taste like the best of summer—sweet on the outside and a surprise of tartness in the center. Delicious!

INGREDIENTS

For the filling
- Lemon Curd (page 111)

For the doughnuts
- 2 tablespoons instant yeast
- 1 cup (240ml) whole milk, warmed
- ½ cup (60g) white bread flour
- 3 cups (375g) all-purpose flour
- ¼ cup (60g) cold unsalted butter, grated
- 2 tablespoons vanilla extract
- 2 large eggs
- 1 large egg yolk
- ¼ cup (50g) superfine sugar, plus extra for dusting
- ½ teaspoon salt
- Vegetable oil for deep-frying

METHOD

Make the lemon curd and chill until needed.

In a bowl, dissolve yeast in milk. Add the bread flour and 1 ½ cups (190g) all-purpose flour. Mix in a stand mixer with the paddle attachment until smooth. Cover and let rest for 20 minutes. Mix in the grated butter, then add the vanilla, eggs, and egg yolk. Turn off mixer, add the sugar and salt, and mix on low until the dough starts to come together. Switching to the dough hook, add the remaining flour in three stages. The dough should pull away from the sides of the bowl, but still be slightly sticky. If it is too wet, add more flour.

Cover and set in a warm place for 30 minutes, then gently press dough down with your fist and leave for 1 hour, or until it has doubled.

Take a tablespoon-size pinch of dough, create an indent in the middle, fill with a small amount of lemon curd, and pinch closed. Leave on a floured parchment-lined cookie sheet for another 15 minutes before frying.

Heat the oil in a heavy, large pan to 360°F (182°C). Cook a few holes at a time for 1 minute on the first side, ½ minute on the second, then remove with a slotted spoon and place on paper towels. While the holes are still warm, shake them in a paper bag filled with sugar.

Makes about 15

POWDERED SUGAR MINIS

Anything but boring, this classic recipe has stood the test of time for a reason.

INGREDIENTS

For the doughnuts
- 1 ½ cups (190g) all-purpose flour
- 1 cup (125g) soy flour
- ½ cup (100g) superfine sugar
- 1 tablespoon baking powder
- ½ teaspoon salt
- 1 teaspoon ground nutmeg
- Pinch ground cinnamon
- 2 tablespoons (30g) cold unsalted butter, grated
- 1 large egg
- ½ cup (120ml) whole milk, warmed
- 2 tablespoons plain yogurt
- 1 tablespoon vanilla extract
- Vegetable oil for deep-frying

For the decoration
- ½ cup (50g) powdered sugar for dusting

METHOD

In a large mixing bowl, sift the flours. Whisk in the baking powder, salt, spices, and sugar. In a stand mixer fitted with the paddle attachment, blend on low. Gradually add the butter and blend until the mixture resembles coarse sand.

In a separate bowl, combine the eggs, ¼ cup (60ml) milk, yogurt, and vanilla. Whisk well. Combine the mixture with the dry ingredients. Blend for 30 seconds and scrape the bowl. Add the remaining milk and mix slowly. The batter should be thick and spoonable. Cover the mixing bowl with plastic wrap and place in the refrigerator for 30 minutes.

Heat the oil in a large, heavy pan to 360°F (182°C). Drop in tablespoon-size portions of the dough and fry for about 1 minute per side, or until golden.

Place paper towels underneath a cooling rack. Remove the holes with a slotted spoon and place them on the rack. Put the powdered sugar inside a small paper bag. While the holes are slightly warm, drop a few inside the bag and shake.

Makes about 15

CHOCOLATE HAZELNUT-FILLED HOLES WITH VANILLA GLAZE

Hazelnut filling is a great alternative to plain chocolate.
Perfect with a morning cup of coffee!

INGREDIENTS

For the doughnuts
- 2 tablespoons instant yeast
- 1 cup (240ml) whole milk, warmed
- ½ cup (60g) white bread flour
- 3 cups (375g) all-purpose flour
- ¼ cup (60g) cold unsalted butter, grated
- 2 tablespoons vanilla extract
- 2 large eggs
- 1 large egg yolk
- ¼ cup (50g) superfine sugar
- ½ teaspoon salt
- Vegetable oil for deep-frying
- ¼ cup (50g) superfine sugar, plus extra for rolling
- ¼ cup (60g) chocolate hazelnut spread

For the glaze
- ¼ cup (25g) powdered sugar, sifted
- ½ tablespoon whole milk
- 1 teaspoon vanilla extract
- 1 vanilla bean

METHOD

In a bowl, dissolve yeast in milk. Add the bread flour and 1 ½ cups (190g) all-purpose flour. Mix in a stand mixer with the paddle attachment until smooth. Cover and let rest for 20 minutes. Mix in the grated butter, then add the vanilla, eggs, and egg yolk. Turn off mixer, add the sugar and salt, and mix on low until the dough starts to come together. Switching to the dough hook, add the remaining flour in three stages. The dough should pull away from the sides of the bowl, but still be slightly sticky. If it is too wet, add a little more flour.

Cover and set in a warm place for 30 minutes, then gently press dough down with your fist and leave for 1 hour, or until it has doubled.

Take a tablespoon-size pinch of dough, create an indent in the middle, fill with a small amount of chocolate hazelnut spread, and pinch closed. Leave on a floured parchment-lined cookie sheet for another 15 minutes before frying.

Heat the oil in a heavy, large pan to 360°F (182°C). Cook a few holes at a time for 1 minute on the first side, ½ minute on the second, then remove with a slotted spoon and place on paper towels.

Make the glaze. In a small bowl, place the powdered sugar, milk, and vanilla extract. Split the vanilla bean lengthwise and use the back of the knife to scrape out half the seeds. Whisk the seeds with the sugar mixture. Dip a spoon into the mixture and allow the mixture to drop off the back of the spoon onto the holes.

Makes about 15

ALMOND DOUGHNUT HOLES WITH CHERRY DIPPING SAUCE

Ahhhh...cherry pie. These doughnut holes taste amazing. Just try not to eat the sauce before the doughnuts are done!

INGREDIENTS

For the doughnuts
- 1 ½ cups (190g) all-purpose flour
- 1 cup (125g) soy flour
- 1 tablespoon baking powder
- ½ teaspoon salt
- 1 teaspoon ground cinnamon
- ½ cup (100g) superfine sugar
- 2 tablespoons (30g) cold unsalted butter, grated
- 1 large egg
- ½ cup (120ml) whole milk, warmed
- 2 tablespoons plain yogurt
- ½ tablespoon almond extract
- Vegetable oil for deep-frying

For the dipping sauce
- ¼ pound (115g) fresh sweet cherries (Bing work best), pitted
- ½ tablespoon lemon juice
- 1 teaspoon superfine sugar
- ¼ tablespoon water
- ½ teaspoon cornstarch
- ½ tablespoon (15g) unsalted butter

METHOD

Sift the flours and whisk in baking powder, salt, cinnamon, and sugar in the bowl of a stand mixer fitted with a paddle attachment. Blend on low. Gradually add the butter and blend until mixture resembles coarse sand.

In a separate bowl, combine the eggs, ¼ cup (60ml) milk, yogurt, and almond extract. Whisk well. Combine with the dry ingredients in the mixing bowl. Blend for 30 seconds and scrape bowl. Add the remaining milk and mix slowly. The batter should be thick and spoonable. Cover bowl with plastic wrap and place in refrigerator for 30 minutes.

Heat the oil in a large, heavy pan to 360°F (182°C). Drop a few tablespoon-size portions of the dough into the oil and fry for approximately 1 minute per side, or until golden and cooked through. Remove with a slotted spoon and place on a cooling rack.

Make the cherry dipping sauce. In a food processor, pulse the pitted cherries with the lemon juice a few times. Scoop the mixture into a pan over medium-high heat. Add sugar and stir until the juices are released. Whisk the water and cornstarch together until blended nicely, add to the cherry mixture, and whisk vigorously. Once thickened, add the butter and stir. Serve immediately alongside warm holes.

Makes about 18

BUTTER PECAN MINI-DOUGHNUTS

Warm brown sugar and toasted pecans remind me of my grandmother. The aroma is amazing and the doughnuts are so gooey when warm.

INGREDIENTS

For the doughnuts
- 2 large eggs
- ¼ cup (50g) superfine sugar
- ¼ cup (50g) brown sugar
- 2 tablespoons active dry yeast
- 2 cups (475ml) whole milk, warmed
- 1 tablespoon vanilla extract
- 1 teaspoon butter flavoring
- 2 teaspoons salt
- 6 cups (750g) all-purpose flour
- 1 cup (230g) cold unsalted butter, grated

For the glaze
- 2 tablespoons (30g) unsalted butter
- ¼ cup (50g) brown sugar
- ½ cup (60g) roasted chopped pecans
- 1 tablespoon hot milk

METHOD

Line two cookie sheets with parchment paper and place paper towels under a cooling rack.

In the bowl of a stand mixer with the paddle attachment, beat eggs and sugars until blended. Add the yeast, milk, vanilla, butter flavoring, and salt, and stir to blend. With the mixer on low, add 4 cups (500g) flour, ½ cup (60g) at a time, until dough pulls away from the sides of the bowl.

Switching to the dough hook, slowly add the grated butter until fully incorporated. On low speed, add the remaining flour. The dough should now be soft, but not too sticky. Knead the dough gently on a lightly floured surface until it is no longer sticky. Butter the inside of a bowl and place the dough ball inside. Cover with plastic wrap and allow the dough to double, about 45 minutes.

Gently press dough down with your fist and roll out ½ inch (1.25cm) thick. Cut out the rounds with a 2 ½-inch (6.5cm) doughnut cutter and set an inch (2.5cm) apart on the parchment-lined cookie sheet. Cover with oiled plastic wrap and let sit until doubled, about 15 minutes.

Preheat oven to 400°F (200°C). Bake doughnuts until they are a light brown, approximately 6–8 minutes. Do not overbake. Remove from the oven, let cool briefly, and transfer to the cooling rack.

For the glaze, melt the butter in a small pan over medium heat. Add the brown sugar and pecans and whisk continually until it starts to boil. Add the milk, then turn the heat to low and whisk 1 more minute. Working quickly, spoon the glaze over the doughnuts. Let set before serving.

Makes about 24

EARL GREY HOLES WITH ORANGE GLAZE

These wonderfully spiced holes pair nicely with their main ingredient, Earl Grey tea.
With the orange zest balancing the spice perfectly, they are great for a morning treat.

INGREDIENTS

For the doughnuts
- 2 tablespoons instant yeast
- ¾ cup (180ml) whole milk, warmed
- ¼ cup (60ml) strong brewed Earl Grey tea, warm
- ½ cup (60g) white bread flour
- 3 cups (375g) all-purpose flour
- ¼ cup (60g) cold unsalted butter, grated
- 2 tablespoons vanilla extract
- 2 large eggs
- 1 large egg yolk
- ¼ cup (50g) superfine sugar
- ½ teaspoon salt
- Vegetable oil for deep-frying

For the glaze
- ¼ cup (60ml) orange juice
- 1 teaspoon freshly grated orange zest
- ¼ cup (25g) powdered sugar

METHOD

In a large mixing bowl, dissolve the yeast in the milk and steeped tea. Add the white bread flour and 1 ½ cups (190g) all-purpose flour. If mixture is too wet, add a little more flour. Mix in a stand mixer with the paddle attachment until smooth. Cover and let rest for 20 minutes.

Gradually add the grated butter to the dough and mix. Add the vanilla, eggs, and egg yolk. Turn off the mixer, add the sugar and salt, then mix on low until the dough starts to come together. Switching to the dough hook attachment, add the remaining flour in three stages. The dough should pull away from the sides of the bowl, but still be slightly sticky. If too wet, add a little more flour. Cover and set in a warm place for 30 minutes. Gently press dough down with your fist and leave again for 1 hour, or until doubled.

Heat the vegetable oil in a heavy, large pan to 360°F (182°C), then fry a few holes at a time for 1 minute on the first side, ½ minute on the second side. Remove with a slotted spoon and place on paper towels to drain.

Make the glaze. In a small bowl, whisk the orange juice, zest, and powdered sugar. The glaze should be thin, but not watery. Add more powdered sugar or orange juice if needed. Using a spoon, drizzle glaze over warm doughnut holes and let set.

Makes about 18

MINI GINGER-LEMON SANDWICHES WITH WHIPPED CREAM FILLING

What could be better than a ladies' brunch with some hot tea and these cute little sandwiches?
Very fancy to eat and very easy to make; just make sure to keep your pinky in the air!

INGREDIENTS

For the doughnuts
- 1 large egg
- 2 tablespoons superfine sugar
- 2 tablespoons brown sugar
- 1 tablespoon active dry yeast
- 1 cup (240ml) whole milk, warmed
- ½ tablespoon vanilla extract
- 1 teaspoon salt
- 1 tablespoon fresh lemon juice
- Freshly grated zest of ½ lemon
- ¾ tablespoon shredded fresh ginger
- 3 cups (375g) all-purpose flour
- ½ cup (115g) cold unsalted butter, grated

For the filling and decoration
- 1 cup (240ml) heavy whipping cream
- Powdered sugar and lemon zest (optional)

METHOD

Line two large cookie sheets with parchment paper.

In the bowl of a stand mixer with the paddle attachment, beat eggs and sugars until blended.

Stir in the yeast, milk, vanilla, and salt. Stir in the lemon juice, lemon zest, and ginger. With the mixer on low, add 2 cups (250g) flour, ½ cup (60g) at a time, until dough pulls from the sides of the bowl. Switching to the dough hook, slowly add the butter until it is fully incorporated. Switching the speed to low, add the remaining flour. The dough should now be soft, but not too sticky.

Knead the dough gently on a lightly floured surface until it is no longer sticky. Butter the inside of a bowl and place the dough ball inside. Cover with plastic wrap and allow the dough to double, about 45 minutes.

Gently press dough down with your fist and roll out to ½-inch (1.25cm) thickness. Cut out the rounds with a 2 ½-inch (6.5cm) round biscuit cutter (no hole in the center). Place an inch (2.5cm) apart on the cookie sheets, cover with oiled plastic wrap, and allow to rise until doubled, about 15 minutes.

Preheat the oven to 350°F (175°C).

Bake doughnuts until they are a light brown, approximately 10 minutes. Be careful not to overbake. Let cool on cookie sheets briefly, then transfer to cooling racks.

For the filling, beat cream until stiff peaks form. When the doughnuts are cool to the touch, cut them in half and place a heaping spoonful of whipped cream in the center. Replace the tops and sprinkle with powdered sugar and lemon zest if you wish.

Makes about 20

Chapter 2

AS FRUITY AS YOU LIKE

With a passing nod to staying healthy, pairing doughnuts with a little fruit
provides a wonderful contrast to the sweetness of the dough, and in this
chapter you will find lots of fruity fillings, frostings, and toppings, with
cake, yeast-raised, and even gluten-free doughnuts.

GLUTEN-FREE APPLE AND CINNAMON FRITTERS

Dust these little fritters with powdered sugar and serve for breakfast, or enjoy for dessert, perhaps with chocolate sauce.

INGREDIENTS

- Vegetable oil for deep-frying
- ½ cup (60g) white rice flour
- 2 tablespoons tapioca flour
- ¼ cup (30g) potato starch
- ½ cup (60g) cornstarch
- 1 teaspoon ground cinnamon
- ½ teaspoon baking powder
- ½ teaspoon baking soda
- ½ teaspoon salt
- 1 large egg, room temperature, lightly beaten
- ½ cup (120ml) whole milk
- 1 ½ cups (150g) peeled, cored, and finely chopped apples (about 3)
- Powdered sugar for dusting

METHOD

Heat the vegetable oil in a heavy, large pan to 360°F (182°C).

While the oil is heating, whisk the flours and starches together in a large bowl with the cinnamon, baking powder, baking soda, and salt. Make a well in the center and add the beaten egg and milk. Mix well to combine. Stir in the chopped apples. Drop generous teaspoons of the apple batter in the oil and cook for 2 minutes on each side, or until golden brown. Drain on paper towels. Serve immediately, dusted with powdered sugar.

Makes about 12

TIP

For a dessert that is not gluten-free, replace the rice flour, potato starch, and tapioca flour with the same amount of all-purpose flour, and serve the fritters with crème pâtissière (pastry cream) for dipping. To make crème pâtissière: Warm 1 ¼ cups (300ml) whole milk in a small pan over a gentle heat. In a medium bowl, whisk ¼ cup (50g) superfine sugar, ¼ cup (60g) flour, 2 teaspoons cornstarch, and 1 beaten egg. Gradually whisk in the warm milk. Return the mixture to the pan, increasing the heat, and stir continuously until it thickens and just begins to boil. Remove from the heat and stir in 1 tablespoon (15g) butter and ½ teaspoon vanilla extract. Cool in the pan, covered with buttered parchment paper to prevent a skin forming. Refrigerate until needed.

BANANA-WALNUT DOUGHNUTS WITH VANILLA FUDGE FROSTING

These are baked banana bread doughnuts with a sweet and salty vanilla fudge icing, a great treat for hungry kids when they come home from school.

INGREDIENTS

For the doughnuts
- ½ cup (60g) all-purpose flour
- ½ cup (60g) whole wheat flour
- ½ cup (100g) brown sugar
- 1 ½ teaspoons ground cinnamon
- 1 teaspoon baking powder
- ¼ teaspoon baking soda
- ½ teaspoon salt
- ½ cup (120ml) buttermilk
- 1 large egg, room temperature, lightly beaten
- 2 tablespoons vegetable oil
- 1 teaspoon vanilla extract
- 2 very ripe bananas, mashed
- ½ cup (60g) chopped walnuts

For the frosting
- ¼ cup (60ml) whole milk
- 1 ½ cups (150g) powdered sugar, sifted
- 6 ounces (170g) vanilla fudge, in small squares
- ½ teaspoon salt

For the decoration
- 3 tablespoons chopped walnuts
- ½ ounce (15g) semisweet chocolate
- 1 tablespoon half-and-half

METHOD

Spray two 6-cup doughnut pans with oil, and preheat the oven to 325°F (160°C).

In a large bowl, whisk together both the flours, brown sugar, cinnamon, baking powder, baking soda, and salt. In a separate bowl, whisk the buttermilk, egg, oil, and vanilla, then pour into the flour mixture. Stir to combine. Add the mashed bananas and walnuts and stir again. Using a disposable pastry bag, pipe the batter into the doughnut pans, three-quarters full, and bake for about 15 minutes, until a toothpick inserted into the center comes out clean. Let cool in the pan for 5 minutes, then transfer to a wire rack to cool.

Make the frosting. Heat the milk until just below a simmer, and gradually add the powdered sugar until it has dissolved. Slowly add the fudge and heat, stirring continuously, until melted. Add the salt and continue to stir until smooth, adding a little more milk if necessary to make the right consistency for frosting. Leave the pan over a very low heat to keep the frosting runny, and stir it occasionally.

Dip half of each doughnut into the frosting and return it to the wire rack to drain. If the frosting thickens, thin it with a little milk. Press a few chopped walnuts around the top of each doughnut. You should have a little frosting left in the pan, so add the semisweet chocolate and thin the frosting with half-and-half to make it the consistency for drizzling. Pour it into a disposable pastry bag, and drizzle back and forth over the doughnuts. Let set before serving.

Makes 12

RHUBARB AND STRAWBERRY CUSTARD DOUGHNUTS

Filled with a compote of rhubarb and strawberries, these doughnuts have crème pâtissière piped into them or you could use whipped cream sweetened with a little sugar.

INGREDIENTS

For the compote
- 3–4 cups (450g–600g) hulled and halved strawberries
- 1–2 cups (150–300g) diced rhubarb
- 1 cup (200g) superfine sugar
- 1 teaspoon ground cinnamon
- ½ teaspoon ground nutmeg
- ¼ teaspoon ground ginger

For the doughnuts
- 1 teaspoon superfine sugar
- ⅔ cup (160ml) whole milk, warmed
- 1 package (2 ¼ teaspoons) active dry yeast
- 3 ½ cups (440g) all-purpose flour
- ⅔ cup (130g) superfine sugar
- 2 teaspoons salt
- 2 large eggs, room temperature, lightly beaten
- ½ cup (115g) salted butter, room temperature, cut into small pieces
- Vegetable oil for deep-frying

For the decoration
- 2 cups (475ml) crème pâtissière (page 29)

METHOD

Cook all the ingredients for the compote over low-medium heat for about 30 minutes, until thick and chunky. Cool.

Line two large cookie sheets with parchment paper.

Stir the teaspoon of sugar into the warm milk, sprinkle with yeast, and leave for 10–15 minutes until frothy.

With the dough hook in the bowl of a stand mixer, stir the flour, ⅔ cup (130g) superfine sugar, and salt. Add the yeast mixture and eggs, and mix until the dough comes together. On medium speed, add the butter a piece at a time, mixing well after each piece. This should take 5–7 minutes. The dough will be sticky, but not very. If too wet, add a little flour; if too dry, add a little water. Transfer to a large oiled bowl, cover, and leave for an hour, until doubled.

Transfer the dough to a lightly floured work surface and punch down. Knead lightly and roll to ½ inch (1.25cm) thick. Cut out rounds with a 2 ½-inch (6.5cm) cutter, place on the cookie sheets, cover with oiled plastic wrap, and rest for an hour.

Heat the oil in a heavy, large pan to 360°F (182°C). Fry the doughnuts for 3 minutes first side, 2 minutes second side. Drain on paper towels, then roll in sugar. Split each one in half horizontally, and place a generous tablespoon of compote in the middle, followed by crème pâtissière piped decoratively in the middle and around the edge. Serve immediately.

Makes 9

PINEAPPLE UPSIDE-DOWN CAKE DOUGHNUTS

We are all familiar with pineapple upside-down cake, and the idea works just as well for doughnuts. It's even better when topped with a caramel-flavored frosting and a candied cherry.

INGREDIENTS

For the topping
- ¼ cup (60g) salted butter
- ½ cup (100g) brown sugar
- 1 (15-ounce/425g) can pineapple rings, drained

For the doughnuts
- ½ cup (115g) salted butter
- ½ cup (100g) superfine sugar
- 1 large egg, room temperature, lightly beaten
- 1 ½ cups (190g) all-purpose flour
- 2 ¼ teaspoons baking powder
- ¼ teaspoon baking soda
- ¼ teaspoon salt
- ½ cup (120ml) buttermilk
- 1 teaspoon vanilla extract

For the frosting
- 2 tablespoons (30g) salted butter
- 2 tablespoons brown sugar
- 2 tablespoons half-and-half (more if needed)
- 1 cup (100g) powdered sugar, sifted

For the decoration
- 12 candied cherries

METHOD

Preheat the oven to 350°F (175°C). Lightly spray two 6-cup doughnut pans with oil. In a small pan, melt the butter over medium heat, add the brown sugar, and stir to dissolve. Place 1 tablespoon in the bottom of each doughnut cup. Slice each pineapple ring in half horizontally to make it thinner and place each one on top of the sugar. Press down lightly.

With an electric mixer, whisk the butter and sugar together until light and fluffy. Add the egg, half at a time, mixing well each time. In a large bowl, whisk the flour, baking powder, baking soda, and salt. Add the flour mix to the butter and sugar alternating with the buttermilk, until fully combined. Add vanilla extract. Either pipe or spoon the batter into the doughnut cups, filling them two-thirds full, and bake for about 20 minutes, or until golden brown and they test done. Carefully run a sharp knife around the edges to loosen the doughnuts and turn them out upside down, so that the pineapple is on the top, onto a wire rack to cool. While the doughnuts are cooling, make the frosting. In a small pan, over a gentle heat, mix the butter and brown sugar, stirring until the sugar is dissolved. Add the half-and-half and powdered sugar a little at a time, until it is all incorporated. When cool enough to handle, thin with a little more half-and-half if necessary. Using a pastry bag or a plastic bag with the corner cut off, drizzle the frosting decoratively around the tops of the doughnuts, and place a candied cherry into the middle of each one. Serve immediately.

Makes 12

BLUEBERRY DOUGHNUT MUFFINS

These little muffins taste just like doughnuts rolled in sugar and conceal a pleasing surprise of delicious blueberry preserves in their center.

INGREDIENTS

- 1 ½ cups (190g) plus 2 tablespoons all-purpose flour
- ¾ cup (150g) superfine sugar
- 1 teaspoon baking powder
- ½ teaspoon baking soda
- ½ teaspoon salt
- 6 tablespoons Greek yogurt
- 2 large eggs, room temperature, lightly beaten
- 1 teaspoon vanilla extract
- ¾ cup (170g) salted butter, melted and cooled slightly
- 12 teaspoons blueberry preserves
- 1 cup (200g) superfine sugar

METHOD

Preheat the oven to 350°F (175°C). Spray a 12-cup muffin pan with oil and line the bases with circles of parchment paper.

In a large bowl, whisk together the flour, sugar, baking powder, baking soda, and salt. In a medium bowl, whisk together the yogurt, eggs, and vanilla extract.

Pour yogurt mixture into the dry ingredients with the melted and cooled butter, and mix until combined. Put 2 tablespoons of the batter into each lined muffin cup. Add 1 teaspoon blueberry preserve to each one and top with the remaining batter.

Bake in the oven for about 20 minutes, until the tops are golden brown. Remove from the oven and let cool in the pan for 10 minutes.

Place the sugar in a wide shallow dish, remove the muffins from the pan, and roll each one in the sugar. Cool on a wire rack. Serve warm.

Makes 12

RASPBERRY DOUGHNUTS WITH SWEET BERRY FROSTING

This baked vanilla doughnut has a crumbly texture because it contains fresh juicy raspberries. It is quite delicate, but utterly delicious.

INGREDIENTS

For the doughnuts
- 2 cups (250g) all-purpose flour
- ¾ cup (150g) superfine sugar
- 2 teaspoons baking powder
- ½ teaspoon baking soda
- ½ teaspoon salt
- 2 large eggs, room temperature
- ¾ cup (180ml) buttermilk
- 2 tablespoons (30g) unsalted butter, melted and cooled slightly
- 1 teaspoon vanilla extract
- ¼ cup (30g) fresh raspberries, halved if large

For the frosting
- ⅓ cup (40g) fresh raspberries
- 1 ½ cups (150g) powdered sugar, sifted

For the decoration
- ¼ cup (80g) semisweet chocolate chips, melted

METHOD

Spray two 6-cup doughnut pans with a little oil. Preheat the oven to 350°F (175°C).

In a large bowl, whisk together the flour, sugar, baking powder, baking soda, and salt. In a separate bowl, whisk the eggs, then add the buttermilk, cooled melted butter, and vanilla extract. Pour egg mixture into the flour mixture and stir until combined. Gently fold in the raspberries. Spoon the batter into the doughnut pans, filling them two-thirds full. Bake for about 10 minutes, or until a toothpick inserted in the center comes out clean. Remove from the oven, let cool in the pans for 5 minutes, and transfer the doughnuts to a wire rack to cool completely.

Make the frosting. Push the fresh raspberries through a sieve into a bowl, leaving just the seeds behind. Slowly add the sifted powdered sugar to the raspberry juice until you have the perfect consistency for dipping. Dip the top of each doughnut into the berry frosting and place back on the rack to drain. When set, drizzle with melted semisweet chocolate before serving.

Makes 12

TIP
Swap frostings! Glaze half the doughnuts with sweet berry frosting, and drizzle with chocolate glaze, and frost the remaining doughnuts with chocolate glaze, drizzled with berry frosting.

STRAWBERRY DOUGHNUTS WITH A HINT OF CORIANDER

If you've never used ground coriander in baking, you'll be very surprised after your first bite of these. It's surprisingly complementary to strawberry. These two ingredients seem like they've been best friends forever.

INGREDIENTS

For the doughnuts
- 1 large egg
- 2 tablespoons superfine sugar
- 2 tablespoons brown sugar
- 1 tablespoon active dry yeast
- 1 cup (240ml) whole milk, warmed
- ½ tablespoon vanilla extract
- 1 teaspoon salt
- ¾ teaspoon ground coriander
- 3 cups (375g) all-purpose flour
- ½ cup (115g) cold unsalted butter, grated

For the glaze
- 3–4 large fresh strawberries
- ¼ tablespoon lemon juice
- ½ cup (50g) powdered sugar, or as needed

METHOD

Cover two large cookie sheets with parchment paper.

In the bowl of a stand mixer with the paddle attachment, beat the eggs and sugars until blended. Add the yeast, milk, vanilla, salt, and coriander. Stir, then add 2 cups (250g) flour, ½ cup (60g) at a time, with the machine on low, until the dough pulls from the sides of the bowl. Switching to the dough hook, slowly add the butter until fully incorporated. Reduce the speed to low and add the remaining flour. The dough should now be soft, but not too sticky. Knead the dough gently on a lightly floured surface until it is no longer sticky. Butter the inside of a bowl and place the dough ball inside. Cover with plastic wrap and allow the dough to double in size, about 45 minutes. Gently press dough down with your fist and roll out ½ inch (1.25cm) thick. Cut out rounds with a 3 ½-inch (8.75cm) doughnut cutter and set an inch (2.5cm) apart on the lined cookie sheets. Cover with oiled plastic wrap and allow to rise until doubled, about 15 minutes.

Preheat oven to 375°F (190°C). Bake until the doughnuts are a light brown, approximately 10–12 minutes. Be careful not to overbake. Let cool for 1 minute, then set on a cooling rack.

For the glaze, mash the strawberries with a fork, then push them through a sieve into a small bowl. (Set aside a few chopped strawberries for a serving garnish.) Add the lemon juice and gradually whisk in the powdered sugar. Use more or less powdered sugar depending on your consistency preference.

Once the doughnuts are cool, dip the top of each one in the glaze and place them on paper towels to set.

Makes about 12

APRICOT DOUGHNUTS WITH WHITE CHOCOLATE DRIZZLE

Warm apricot and white chocolate are a dream together! The white chocolate lends a sweetness, whereas the apricots add tartness. Perfection!

INGREDIENTS

For the doughnuts
- 1 large egg
- 2 tablespoons superfine sugar
- 2 tablespoons brown sugar
- 1 tablespoon active dry yeast
- 1 cup (240ml) whole milk, warmed
- ½ tablespoon vanilla extract
- 1 teaspoon salt
- 3 cups (375g) all-purpose flour
- ½ cup (115g) cold unsalted butter, grated
- ¾ cup (100g) chopped dried apricots

For the glaze
- 1 ½ tablespoons apricot preserves

For the decoration
- ¼ cup (80g) white chocolate chips
- ½ tablespoon whole milk
- Several dried apricots, finely chopped

METHOD

Cover two large cookie sheets with parchment paper.

In the bowl of a stand mixer with the paddle attachment, beat the eggs and sugars until blended. Add the yeast, vanilla, milk, and salt. Stir, then add 2 cups (250g) flour, ½ cup (60g) at a time, with the machine on low, until the dough pulls from the sides of the bowl. Switching to the dough hook, slowly add the butter until fully incorporated. Reduce the speed to low and add the remaining flour. Add the chopped apricots and mix for 10 seconds. The dough should now be soft, but not too sticky.

Knead the dough gently on a lightly floured surface until it is no longer sticky. Butter the inside of a bowl and place the dough ball inside. Cover with plastic wrap and allow the dough to double, about 45 minutes. Gently press dough down with your fist and roll out ½ inch (1.25cm) thick. Cut out rounds with a 3 ½-inch (8.75cm) doughnut cutter and set an inch (2.5cm) apart on the cookie sheets. Cover with oiled plastic wrap and allow to rise until doubled, about 15 minutes.

Preheat oven to 375°F (190°C). Bake until doughnuts are light brown, approximately 10–12 minutes. Be careful not to overbake. Let cool on the pans for 1 minute, then transfer to a cooling rack.

Make the glaze. Heat the apricot preserves until the consistency is slightly runny. Brush it over the tops of the warm doughnuts with a pastry brush so it is absorbed.

To finish, in a microwave-safe bowl, combine the white chocolate chips and milk. Heat in the microwave for 30-second intervals, stirring between intervals, until smooth. Working quickly, as the chocolate will harden, use a fork to drizzle over doughnuts. Sprinkle the tops with finely chopped dried apricots.

Makes about 12

APPLE CIDER DOUGHNUTS WITH MAPLE CREAM GLAZE

The perfect pairing to this fall doughnut is a hayride and mittens.
For an extra treat, dunk in hot cocoa and smile.

INGREDIENTS

For the doughnuts
- 1 cup (240ml) apple cider
- 3 ½ cups (440g) all-purpose flour
- 2 teaspoons baking powder
- 1 teaspoon baking soda
- ½ teaspoon salt
- ½ teaspoon ground cinnamon
- ¼ teaspoon ground nutmeg
- Pinch ground black pepper
- Pinch ground cardamom
- ¼ cup (60g) cold unsalted butter, grated
- 1 cup (200g) superfine sugar
- ¼ teaspoon vanilla extract
- 2 large eggs
- ½ cup (120ml) buttermilk
- Vegetable oil for deep-frying

For the glaze
- ½ cup (50g) powdered sugar
- 2 tablespoons maple syrup
- 2 tablespoons heavy cream
- ¼ teaspoon maple flavoring
- Pinch salt

METHOD

Reduce the cider down to ¼ cup (60ml) in a saucepan over medium-low heat (approximately 20–30 minutes) and let cool.

Combine the flour, baking powder, baking soda, salt, cinnamon, nutmeg, black pepper, and cardamom. Set aside.

With an electric mixer, beat the butter, sugar, and vanilla until smooth. Add the eggs, one at a time, until completely incorporated. Gradually add the cooled reduced cider and the buttermilk until just combined. Slowly add the flour mixture and mix until the dough comes together. Refrigerate the dough for 20 minutes (or it can be refrigerated overnight).

Roll out dough to ¾-inch (2cm) thickness. Cut out doughnuts with a 3 ½-inch (8.75cm) doughnut cutter and place on floured parchment paper-lined cookie sheets. Heat the oil in a heavy, large pan to 360°F (182°C). Fry a few doughnuts at a time for 2 minutes on each side. Remove doughnuts and place on paper towels to drain.

Make the glaze by whisking together the ingredients in a bowl. If consistency is too thin, add more powdered sugar; if too thick, add more cream. While the doughnuts are still warm, drizzle glaze across the tops using a fork. Let set before serving.

Makes about 15

VEGAN BANANA CLOVE FRITTERS

Nothing could be better than sweet banana, spicy cloves, and the perfect crunchy outside.
Except for the fact that these are vegan!

INGREDIENTS

- 3 ⅓ cups (450g) mashed ripe bananas
- 6 tablespoons brown sugar
- 2 tablespoons superfine sugar
- 1 ½ teaspoons ground cloves
- 1 teaspoon vanilla extract
- 2 cups (250g) all-purpose flour
- Pinch salt
- Vegetable oil for shallow-frying
- Powdered sugar for dusting

METHOD

In a medium bowl, mix bananas, sugars, ground cloves, and vanilla. Add the flour and salt.

Place a large pan on the stove over medium-high heat. Cover the bottom with vegetable oil. Once the pan is hot, place a couple of large spoonfuls of batter into the pan and press them into 3-inch (7.5cm) patties. Let brown on each side, about 1 minute.

Remove from pan and place on paper towels to drain. Sprinkle tops with powdered sugar and enjoy while still warm.

Makes about 36

LIME POPPY SEED DOUGHNUTS WITH KEY LIME GLAZE

The perfect pairing of tart and sweet, these doughnuts feel at home next to a margarita! Fresh Key lime juice is preferable, but bottled Key lime juice will work.

INGREDIENTS

For the doughnuts
- 4 ½ cups (560g) all-purpose flour
- 4 teaspoons baking powder
- 2 teaspoons salt
- 1 ½ cups (300g) superfine sugar
- 3 tablespoons poppy seeds
- 4 large eggs
- 1 ¼ cups (300ml) whole milk
- ¼ cup (60ml) freshly squeezed Key lime juice
- 2 tablespoons (30g) cold unsalted butter, grated
- 1 teaspoon vanilla extract
- 1 tablespoon Key lime zest

For the glaze
- 2 cups (200g) powdered sugar
- 2 tablespoons Key lime juice
- 1 teaspoon light corn syrup
- 2 teaspoons Key lime zest

METHOD

Preheat the oven to 350°F (175°C). Using a nonstick spray, spray two 12-cup doughnut pans.

In a large bowl, sift together the flour, baking powder, and salt. Whisk in sugar and poppy seeds.

In the bowl of a stand mixer fitted with a paddle attachment, mix the eggs, milk, lime juice, butter, vanilla, and zest. Slowly add the flour mixture until smooth.

Place the batter in a pastry bag or a plastic bag with the corner cut off and pipe into the doughnut baking cups, filling them three-quarters full. Bake until light golden brown, about 10–12 minutes. Let cool in the pans for a few minutes, then carefully transfer to a wire rack until slightly warm.

Make the glaze. Whisk together the powdered sugar, lime juice, corn syrup, and zest. If glaze is too thin, add more powdered sugar; if it is too thick, add more lime juice. Place glaze in a small bowl and dip the tops of the doughnuts to cover. Place doughnuts on paper towels to dry before serving.

Makes about 24–30

COCONUT DOUGHNUTS WITH TROPICAL GLAZE

Coconut milk creates the most amazing creamy texture in this doughnut, while the glaze is the perfect sweet complement. Also looks great next to a drink with an umbrella!

INGREDIENTS

For the doughnuts
- 2 tablespoons active-dry yeast
- 1 cup (240ml) canned coconut milk, warmed
- ½ cup (60g) white bread flour
- 3 cups (375g) all-purpose flour
- ¼ cup (60g) cold unsalted butter, grated
- 2 tablespoons vanilla extract
- 2 large eggs
- 1 large egg yolk
- ¼ cup (50g) superfine sugar
- ½ teaspoon salt
- Vegetable oil for deep-frying

For the glaze
- 1 cup (100g) powdered sugar
- 1 tablespoon light rum
- ½ tablespoon pineapple juice
- ½ teaspoon corn syrup

For the decoration
- ¼ cup (30g) coconut flakes

METHOD

In a bowl, dissolve the yeast in the coconut milk. Let stand until frothy, 10–15 minutes. Add the bread flour and 1 ½ cups (190g) all-purpose flour. Mix in a stand mixer with the paddle attachment until smooth. Cover and let rest for 20 minutes.

Gradually add the grated butter to the dough and mix until combined. Then add the vanilla, eggs, and egg yolk. Turn off the mixer and add the sugar and salt, then mix on low until the dough starts to come together.

Switching to the dough hook attachment, add the remaining flour in three stages. The dough should pull away from the sides of the bowl nicely, but still be slightly sticky. If too sticky, add a little more flour. Cover and set in a warm place for 30 minutes. Gently press the dough down with your fist and let sit again for 1 hour, or until the dough has doubled in size. Turn the dough out onto a lightly floured surface and roll ½ inch (1.25cm) thick. Cut doughnuts using a 3 ½-inch (8.75cm) doughnut cutter, place an inch (2.5cm) apart on floured cookie sheets, cover with oiled plastic wrap, and allow to rise for 15 minutes.

Heat the oil in a heavy, large pan to 360°F (182°C). Fry doughnuts for 2 minutes on each side, then remove with a slotted spoon and place on paper towels. Let cool while making the glaze.

Make the glaze by whisking the ingredients together in a bowl until smooth. Using a fork, drizzle the glaze over the doughnuts. Spread out the coconut on a cookie sheet and bake for 6–7 minutes, until lightly toasted, but not burned. Watch it carefully and stir once or twice during cooking. When the glaze is almost set, sprinkle with the coconut flakes.

Makes about 15

CRANBERRY DOUGHNUTS WITH ORANGE GLAZE

One bite of these spiced doughnuts, and you'll be able to feel the cool fall wind and hear leaves rustling. They are pretty enough to serve with holiday meals, too!

INGREDIENTS

For the doughnuts
- 3 cups (375g) all-purpose flour
- 2 teaspoons baking powder
- 1 teaspoon baking soda
- ½ teaspoon salt
- 1 teaspoon ground cinnamon
- ¾ cup (85g) cold unsalted butter, grated
- 1 ¾ cups (350g) superfine sugar
- 3 large eggs
- 1 teaspoon vanilla extract
- ¾ cup (180ml) buttermilk (or just under ¾ cup (180ml) whole milk and 2 tablespoons white vinegar)
- 1 cup (120g) dried cranberries
- ½ cup (120ml) fresh orange juice

For the glaze
- 2 cups (200g) powdered sugar, sifted
- 3 tablespoons fresh orange juice
- 2 teaspoons freshly grated orange zest, plus more for decoration
- 1 tablespoon (15g) melted unsalted butter

METHOD

Using a nonstick spray, spray two 12-cup doughnut pans. Preheat oven to 350°F (175°C).

In a medium bowl, combine flour, baking powder, baking soda, salt, and cinnamon until incorporated. Using a stand mixer with a paddle attachment, cream the butter and sugar until well blended. Add the eggs one at a time, scraping between additions. Add the vanilla. Alternately add the flour mixture and the buttermilk to the egg mixture, ending with the flour. Scrape down sides of the bowl.

In a microwave-safe bowl, combine the cranberries and orange juice. Microwave for 45 seconds and let sit for 5 minutes. Add the cranberry mixture to the batter and mix for 10 seconds.

Fill doughnut cups three-quarters full with the batter. Bake for 10–12 minutes or until a toothpick inserted in the center comes out clean. Cool in the pans for a few minutes, then carefully transfer to a wire rack to fully cool.

Make the glaze. Whisk together the powdered sugar, orange juice and zest, and melted butter. Add more powdered sugar if the glaze is too thin. Dip the tops of the doughnuts in the glaze and return to the cooling rack. When the glaze is almost set, decorate the tops with extra orange zest.

Makes about 30

LINGONBERRY DOUGHNUTS WITH ALMOND DRIZZLE

These doughnuts give a nod to the Scandinavian fruit, the lingonberry. They pop in your mouth with a slight sour/sweet taste and when paired with almond flavoring, they are heavenly!

INGREDIENTS

For the doughnuts
- 2 tablespoons active-dry yeast
- 1 cup (240ml) whole milk, warmed
- ½ cup (60g) white bread flour
- 3 cups (375g) all-purpose flour
- ¼ cup (60g) cold unsalted butter, grated
- 1 teaspoon almond extract
- 2 large eggs
- 1 large egg yolk
- ¼ cup (50g) superfine sugar
- ½ teaspoon salt
- Vegetable oil for deep-frying

For the lingonberry glaze
- 1 cup (340g) lingonberry preserves
- 1 teaspoon light corn syrup

For the almond glaze
- ½ cup (50g) powdered sugar, sifted
- 1½ tablespoons heavy cream
- 1 teaspoon almond extract

For the decoration (optional)
- Slivered almonds

METHOD

In a bowl, dissolve the yeast in the milk. Add the bread flour and 1 ½ cups (190g) all-purpose flour. Mix in a stand mixer with the paddle attachment until smooth. Cover and let rest for 20 minutes. Gradually add the grated butter and mix until combined. Add the almond extract, eggs, and egg yolk. Turn off the mixer and add the sugar and salt. Mix on low until the dough starts to come together. Switching to the dough hook attachment, add the remaining flour in three stages. The dough should pull away from the sides of the bowl nicely, but still be slightly sticky. If too sticky, add a little more flour. Cover and set in a warm place for 30 minutes.

Gently press dough down with your fist and let sit again for 1 hour, or until the dough has doubled in size. On a lightly floured surface, roll dough ½ inch (1.25cm) thick. Cut rounds using a 3 ½-inch (8.75cm) doughnut cutter, place 1 inch (2.5cm) apart on floured cookie sheets, cover with oiled plastic wrap, and allow to rise for 15 minutes.

Heat the oil in a large, heavy pan to 360°F (182°C). Fry a few doughnuts at a time for 2 minutes per side, then remove with a slotted spoon and place on paper towels to cool.

Make the lingonberry glaze in a small saucepan over low heat by mixing the preserves and corn syrup. After the glaze becomes thin, remove from heat. Make the almond drizzle glaze by whisking together the ingredients in a small bowl.

Once the doughnuts are cool, dip the top of each one in the lingonberry glaze, then place on paper towels to set slightly. Drizzle the almond glaze decoratively on top. For an extra pretty look, sprinkle slivered almonds on top.

Makes about 15

VEGAN SPICED PEAR SANDWICH WITH CINNAMON DRIZZLE

Don't think it's possible for a treat to be decadent AND vegan? Biting into these little jewels will feel like you're rewarding yourself for something. Go ahead...it's OK.

INGREDIENTS

For the doughnuts
- 1 ¼ tablespoons cornstarch
- 1 ¼ tablespoons potato starch
- Heaping ¼ teaspoon baking powder
- ½ cup (60ml) water
- 1 teaspoon vegetable oil
- 2 tablespoons active dry yeast
- 1 cup (240ml) soy milk, warmed
- ½ cup (60g) white bread flour
- 3 cups (375g) all-purpose flour
- ¼ teaspoon ground cinnamon
- ⅛ teaspoon ground nutmeg
- ⅛ teaspoon ground black pepper
- Pinch ground cardamom
- ¼ cup (50g) vegetable shortening
- ½ tablespoon vanilla extract
- ¼ cup (50g) superfine sugar
- ½ teaspoon salt
- Vegetable oil for deep-frying

For the filling
- 3 large peeled, cored pears
- 1 ½ tablespoons lemon juice
- ½ cup (100g) brown sugar
- ¼ tablespoon ground cinnamon
- Pinch ground nutmeg
- Pinch black pepper
- 1 ½ tablespoons cornstarch

For the glaze
- 1 cup (100g) powdered sugar
- 1 ½ tablespoons soy milk
- ½ teaspoon ground cinnamon
- 1 drop cinnamon oil

METHOD

Whisk together the cornstarch, potato starch, and baking powder. Whisk in water and oil and incorporate fully. This is the egg replacer.

In a mixing bowl, dissolve yeast in soy milk. Add the bread flour, 1 ½ cups (190g) all-purpose flour, and spices. Mix in a stand mixer with the paddle attachment until smooth. Cover and leave for 20 minutes. Mix in shortening, then vanilla and egg replacer. Turn off mixer, add sugar and salt, then mix on low until the dough starts to come together.

Using the dough hook, add the remaining flour in three stages. The dough should pull away from the sides of the bowl, but still be slightly sticky. If too sticky, add more flour; if too dry, add more milk. Cover and set in a warm place for 30 minutes. Gently press dough down with your fist and rest again for 1 hour, or until doubled.

On a lightly floured surface, roll dough ½ inch (1.25cm) thick. Cut rounds with a 3 ½-inch (8.75cm) biscuit cutter (no hole in center). Heat the oil in a heavy, large pan to 360°F (182°C) and fry a few rounds at a time for 3 minutes on the first side, and 2 minutes on the second side. Remove with a slotted spoon, let drain on paper towels, and cool on a cooling rack. Slice almost completely in half.

Make the filling. Toss the pears with lemon juice in a saucepan and cook, stirring, over medium-high heat for 6 minutes. Whisk together brown sugar, cinnamon, nutmeg, black pepper, and cornstarch, and add to pears. Stir for 2 minutes until thickened. Remove from heat and let sit for 5 minutes before filling doughnuts. Any remaining pear filling can be chilled for up to 1 week.

Make the glaze by whisking together all the ingredients, then drizzle over doughnuts using a fork.

Makes about 15

Chapter 3

STUFFED WITH ANYTHING

Very versatile, doughnuts are delicious stuffed with just about anything.
The different combinations are endless—only limited by your imagination
and inventiveness. Start with the ideas in this chapter, and then
try swapping the toppings and fillings around according to your
personal preferences.

BOSTON CREAM DOUGHNUTS

Filled with crème pâtissière and smothered in a rich chocolate glaze, these Boston cream doughnuts will have your friends lining up at the door.

INGREDIENTS

For the doughnuts
- ⅓ cup (80ml) warm water
- 1 teaspoon superfine sugar
- 1 package (2 ¼ teaspoons) active dry yeast
- 3 cups (375g) all-purpose flour
- ¾ cup (90g) white bread flour
- ½ cup (100g) superfine sugar
- 2 teaspoons salt
- ⅓ cup (80ml) whole milk, warmed
- 2 large eggs, room temperature, lightly beaten
- ½ cup (115g) salted butter, room temperature, cut into small pieces
- 1 quantity crème pâtissière (page 29)
- Vegetable oil for deep-frying

For the glaze
- 4 tablespoons unsweetened cocoa powder, sifted
- 2–3 tablespoons whole milk
- 1 teaspoon vanilla extract
- 1 ½ cups (150g) powdered sugar, sifted

For the decoration
- ½ cup (160g) white chocolate chips

METHOD

Line two large cookie sheets with parchment paper.

Place the warm water in a medium bowl, stir in the teaspoon of sugar and the yeast, and leave for 10–15 minutes.

With the dough hook in the bowl of a stand mixer, stir both flours, ½ cup (100g) superfine sugar, and salt together. Add the yeast liquid, warm milk, and beaten eggs, and mix until the dough comes together. On medium speed, add the butter in small pieces, ensuring each piece is fully incorporated before you add the next piece, about 5–7 minutes. The dough should be slightly sticky. If it is too wet, add more flour; too dry, add more water. Transfer to a lightly oiled bowl, cover, and leave for an hour, until doubled.

Transfer the dough to a lightly floured work surface, knead twice, divide into 15 equal pieces, and flatten each one out. Spoon a generous teaspoon of crème pâtissière into the middle of each piece and fold up the dough around the filling, sealing well. Place an inch (2.5cm) apart on the cookie sheets, seam underneath, cover with oiled plastic wrap, and leave for 20 minutes.

Heat the oil in a heavy, large pan to 360°F (182°C). Fry the doughnuts for 3 minutes on the first side, 2 minutes on the second. Drain on paper towels, then cool on a wire rack.

Make the glaze. Warm the milk and vanilla gently in a small pan, stir in the cocoa powder, and gradually add the powdered sugar until you get a slightly runny consistency for dipping. Dip the tops of the doughnuts into the glaze and place back on the wire rack to cool and set. When almost set, decorate with white chocolate chips.

Makes 15

CHERRY DOUGHNUTS WITH STRAWBERRY FROSTING AND WHITE CHOCOLATE CHIPS

With a sweet dark cherry filling, and strawberry and white chocolate topping, these doughnuts fit the bill.

INGREDIENTS

For the doughnuts
- ⅓ cup (80ml) warm water
- 1 teaspoon superfine sugar
- 1 package (2 ¼ teaspoons) active dry yeast
- 3 cups (375g) all-purpose flour
- ¾ cup (90g) white bread flour
- ½ cup (100g) superfine sugar
- 2 teaspoons salt
- ⅓ cup (80ml) whole milk, warmed
- 2 large eggs, room temperature, lightly beaten
- ½ cup (115g) salted butter, room temperature, cut into small pieces
- ½ cup (170g) dark cherry preserves
- Vegetable oil for deep-frying

For the frosting
- 2 teaspoons strawberry preserves
- 1 teaspoon water
- ¾ cup (75g) powdered sugar, sifted
- ½ tablespoon whole milk
- 1 drop red food coloring (optional)
- ½ cup (160g) white chocolate chips

METHOD

Line two large cookie sheets with parchment paper.

Place the warm water in a medium bowl, stir in the teaspoon of sugar and yeast, and leave for 10–15 minutes.

With the dough hook in the bowl of a stand mixer, stir both the flours, ½ cup (100g) superfine sugar, and salt together. Add the yeast liquid, warm milk, and beaten eggs, and mix until the dough comes together. On medium speed, gradually add the small pieces of butter, mixing well each time. The dough should be slightly sticky. If it is too wet, add more flour; too dry, add more water. Transfer to a lightly oiled bowl, cover, and leave for an hour.

Transfer dough to a lightly floured work surface, knead twice, divide into 15 equal pieces, and flatten out each piece. Spoon a generous teaspoon of dark cherry preserves into the middle of each piece and fold up the dough around the filling, sealing well. Place an inch (2.5cm) apart on the cookie sheets, seam underneath, cover with oiled plastic wrap, and leave for 20 minutes.

Heat the oil in a heavy, large pan to 360°F (182°C). Fry the doughnuts for 3 minutes on the first side, 2 minutes on the second. Drain on paper towels, then cool on a wire rack.

Make the frosting. Warm the preserves and 1 teaspoon water over a gentle heat. Push mixture through a sieve into a small bowl to remove seeds. Mix in the powdered sugar and enough milk to make a dipping consistency. If desired, add a drop of red food coloring. Dip the top of each doughnut in the glaze and return to the wire rack to cool and set. When almost set, decorate with white chocolate chips.

Makes 15

CHOCOLATE BOURBON CREAM WITH CHOCOLATE GANACHE AND PISTACHIO SPRINKLE

Use your favorite bourbon (or espresso if you prefer) for the filling of these rich and chocolatey doughnuts. You can increase the amount of bourbon, if you like, by reducing the half-and-half by the same amount.

INGREDIENTS

For the filling
- 6 ounces (170g) semisweet chocolate, broken into pieces
- ¼ cup (60ml) half-and-half
- 1 egg yolk
- 1 tablespoon bourbon (or espresso coffee)

For the doughnuts
- ⅓ cup (80ml) warm water
- 1 teaspoon superfine sugar
- 1 package (2 ¼ teaspoons) active dry yeast
- 3 cups (375g) all-purpose flour
- ¾ cup (90g) white bread flour
- ½ cup (100g) superfine sugar
- 2 teaspoons salt
- ⅓ cup (80ml) whole milk, warmed
- 2 large eggs, room temperature, lightly beaten
- ½ cup (115g) salted butter, room temperature, cut into small pieces
- Vegetable oil for deep-frying

For the ganache
- 8 ounces (225g) unsweetened chocolate, chopped
- 1 cup (240ml) heavy cream

For the decoration
- ½ cup (60g) chopped pistachio nuts

METHOD

Line two large cookie sheets with parchment paper.

Make the bourbon cream filling. Heat the chocolate in the half-and-half in a small pan over very low heat until melted. Add the egg yolk and whisk for 1 minute to keep it from sticking or forming lumps, then remove from heat and stir in bourbon. Set aside to cool.

Place the warm water in a medium bowl, stir in the teaspoon of sugar and the yeast, and leave for 10–15 minutes.

With the dough hook in the bowl of a stand mixer, stir both the flours, ½ cup (100g) superfine sugar, and salt together. Add the yeast liquid, warm milk, and beaten eggs, and mix until the dough comes together. On medium speed, gradually add the pieces of butter, mixing well each time. The dough should be slightly sticky. If it is too wet, add more flour; too dry, add more water. Transfer to a lightly oiled bowl, cover, and leave for an hour.

Transfer dough to a lightly floured work surface, knead twice, divide into 15 equal pieces, and flatten out each piece. Spoon a generous teaspoon of bourbon cream into the middle of each piece and fold up the dough around the filling, sealing well. Place an inch (2.5cm) apart on the cookie sheets, seam underneath, cover with oiled plastic wrap, and leave for 20 minutes.

Heat the oil in a heavy, large pan to 360°F (182°C). Fry the doughnuts for 3 minutes on the first side, 2 minutes on the second. Drain on paper towels, then cool on a wire rack.

Make the chocolate ganache. Place the chopped chocolate in a small bowl. Heat the heavy cream until just boiling. Remove from the heat and pour over the chocolate. Leave for a few minutes until the chocolate has melted, then stir until smooth. Dip the top of each doughnut in the ganache, and when almost set, decorate with chopped pistachio nuts.

Makes 15

CRODOUGHS WITH CRÈME PÂTISSIÈRE AND RASPBERRY FROSTING

A hybrid pastry that marries the texture of a flaky buttery croissant, with the satisfactory bite of a deep-fried doughnut, these delectable little morsels are highly addictive.

INGREDIENTS

For the doughnuts
- ⅓ cup (80ml) whole milk, warmed
- 1 teaspoon superfine sugar
- 1 package (2 ¼ teaspoons) active dry yeast
- 1 ⅓ cups (170g) white bread flour, divided
- 2 tablespoons superfine sugar
- 1 large egg, room temperature, lightly beaten
- 1 tablespoon unsalted butter, softened
- 1 cup (125g) all-purpose flour
- 1 teaspoon salt
- ½ cup (115g) unsalted butter, very cold, cut into cubes
- Vegetable oil for deep-frying
- 1 cup (200g) superfine sugar (for rolling)
- 1 quantity crème pâtissière (page 29)

For the frosting
- ¾ cup (75g) powdered sugar, sifted
- 1 tablespoon whole milk
- 2 teaspoons smooth raspberry preserves

For the decoration
- ¼ cup (30g) sliced almonds

METHOD

Line a large cookie sheet with parchment paper.

Place the warm milk in a medium bowl, stir in the teaspoon of sugar and the yeast, and leave for 10–15 minutes. Add ⅓ bread flour and beat well. Add 2 tablespoons superfine sugar and the egg, and beat again until smooth. Add 1 tablespoon softened butter, beat, and set aside. Put remaining flour and salt into the bowl of a food processor, add the cold butter, and pulse briefly until butter is the size of peas. Tip mixture into a medium-sized bowl, add milk and yeast mixture, and mix until moistened. Cover bowl and refrigerate for 2 hours.

Remove the bowl from the refrigerator, transfer dough onto a lightly floured surface, and knead lightly. Roll dough into a 15 x 5-inch (40 x 12cm) rectangle, then fold into thirds, bringing the bottom third up and folding the top third down. Put into a greased plastic bag and refrigerate for 1 hour. Repeat the rolling and chilling twice more. You can leave the dough in the refrigerator overnight at this stage.

Roll out the dough 1 ½ inches (3.75cm) thick, and using a 3 ½-inch (8.75cm) doughnut cutter, cut 6 or 7 rounds. Reroll the dough as necessary. Set the rounds an inch (2.5cm) apart on the cookie sheet, and cover with oiled plastic wrap. Chill for 1 hour.

Heat the oil in a heavy, large pan to 360°F (182°C). Fry the pastries for 3 minutes on the first side, 2 minutes on the second. Drain on paper towels, and roll in sugar. Cool on a wire rack.

Pipe the crème pâtissière around the middle of each pastry, between the flaky layers, twice, to have two levels of cream.

Make the frosting. Mix the powdered sugar, milk, and preserves until smooth. Pipe or spread a little around the top of each pastry, and decorate with a few sliced almonds, if desired. Serve immediately.

Makes 6–7

GOOEY S'MORES

*These chocolate-topped s'mores doughnuts are filled with a gooey marshmallow
and a rich chocolate cream that oozes out as you bite into them.*

INGREDIENTS

For the doughnuts
- ⅓ cup (80ml) warm water
- 1 teaspoon superfine sugar
- 1 package (2 ¼ teaspoons) active dry yeast
- 3 cups (375g) all-purpose flour
- ¾ cup (90g) white bread flour
- ½ cup (100g) superfine sugar
- 2 teaspoons salt
- ⅓ cup (80ml) whole milk, warmed
- 2 large eggs, room temperature, lightly beaten
- ½ cup (115g) salted butter, room temperature, cut into small pieces
- Vegetable oil for deep-frying

For the glaze
- ¼ cup (60ml) whole milk
- ½ cup (160g) semisweet chocolate chips
- ¼ cup (25g) powdered sugar, sifted
- 3 graham crackers, crushed

For the chocolate filling
- 6 ounces (170g) semisweet chocolate, broken into pieces
- ½ cup (120ml) heavy cream

For the marshmallow filling
- 1 cup (240ml) marshmallow fluff
- 4 ounces (115g) cream cheese
- 1 cup (100g) powdered sugar, sifted

METHOD

Line two large cookie sheets with parchment paper.

Place the warm water in a medium bowl, stir in the teaspoon of sugar and the yeast, and leave for 10–15 minutes.

With the dough hook in the bowl of a stand mixer, stir both the flours, ½ cup (100g) superfine sugar, and salt together. Add the yeast liquid, warm milk, and eggs, and mix until the dough comes together. On medium speed, gradually add the pieces of butter, mixing well each time. The dough should be slightly sticky. If too wet, add more flour; too dry, add more water. Transfer to a lightly oiled bowl, cover, and leave for an hour.

Transfer dough to a lightly floured work surface, knead twice, and roll out to a thickness of ½ inch (1.25cm). Cut out 12 doughnuts, using a 3 ½-inch (8.75cm) cutter, and place an inch (2.5cm) apart on the cookie sheets. Cover with oiled plastic wrap and leave for an hour.

Heat the oil in a heavy, large pan to 360°F (182°C). Fry the doughnuts for 3 minutes on the first side, 2 minutes on the second. Drain on paper towels, and cool on a wire rack.

Make the glaze. Heat the milk until it is scalding hot. Remove from heat and whisk in chocolate chips and powdered sugar until smooth. Dip top of each doughnut into the topping and return to the wire rack to set. Make the chocolate filling. Place the chopped chocolate in a small bowl. Heat the heavy cream until just boiling, pour over the chocolate, and stir until smooth.

Make the marshmallow filling. Beat the marshmallow fluff, cream cheese, and powdered sugar until smooth. Carefully slice the doughnuts almost in half horizontally, and fill each with a tablespoon of marshmallow filling and a teaspoon of chocolate cream filling. Try not to disturb the chocolate topping. Sprinkle tops with crushed graham crackers. Serve immediately.

Makes about 12

PRALINE CREAM DOUGHNUTS WITH SALTED CARAMEL FROSTING

The praline cream in these beauties is what really makes them amazing.
You just might find yourself eating the filling out of the pan!

INGREDIENTS

For the filling
- 3 large egg yolks
- ¼ cup (50g) brown sugar
- ⅙ cup (20g) cornstarch
- ¼ teaspoon ground cinnamon
- Pinch salt
- 1 cup (240ml) heavy cream
- ½ teaspoon vanilla extract
- 2 tablespoons (30g) cold unsalted butter, cubed
- 1 cup (125g) chopped toasted pecans

For the doughnuts
- 2 tablespoons active dry yeast
- 1 cup (240ml) whole milk, warmed
- ½ cup (60g) white bread flour
- 3 cups (375g) all-purpose flour
- ¼ cup (60g) cold unsalted butter, grated

- 1 teaspoon vanilla extract
- 2 large eggs
- 1 large egg yolk
- 2 tablespoons plain yogurt
- ¼ cup (50g) superfine sugar
- ½ teaspoon salt
- Vegetable oil for deep-frying

For the frosting
- 2 ½ tablespoons (40g) unsalted butter
- ¼ cup (60ml) heavy cream
- ¼ cup (50g) superfine sugar
- ¼ cup (50g) brown sugar
- ¼ teaspoon salt
- ½ cup (50g) powdered sugar
- Fleur de sel (or plain sea salt) for sprinkling

METHOD

Make the praline cream filling. In a saucepan (without heat), whisk yolks, brown sugar, cornstarch, cinnamon, and salt until blended. Bring cream just to a boil, then pour very slowly into egg mixture, whisking constantly, to temper eggs. Still whisking, bring to a boil. Once boiling, stir for 1 minute, remove, and whisk in vanilla. Let rest for 5 minutes, then whisk in butter. Stir in pecans. Let cool, press plastic wrap smoothly on the top to prevent a film, and chill.

In a large bowl, dissolve yeast in milk. Add bread flour and 1 ½ cups (190g) all-purpose flour. Mix in a stand mixer with paddle attachment until smooth. Cover and let rest for 20 minutes. Gradually add butter and mix until incorporated. Add vanilla, eggs, egg yolk, and yogurt. Turn off mixer, add sugar and salt, then mix on low until dough starts to come together.

With the dough hook, add remaining flour in three stages. The dough should pull away from the sides of the bowl, but still be still be slightly sticky. If too wet, add a little flour. Cover and set in a warm place for 30 minutes. Gently press dough down and let sit for 1 hour, or until doubled. On a lightly floured surface, roll dough ½ inch (1.25cm) thick. Cut rounds with a 3 ½-inch (8.75cm) biscuit cutter, place on floured cookie sheets, cover with oiled plastic wrap, and let rise for 15 minutes.

Make frosting. Over medium heat, combine butter, cream, sugar, brown sugar, and salt. Bring to a low boil, stir occasionally for 2 minutes, remove, and let cool. When cooled, beat in powdered sugar until smooth.

Heat oil in a large, heavy pan to 360°F (182°C). Fry doughnuts for 3 minutes on first side, then 2 minutes on the other side, remove, and drain on paper towels. To serve, cut cooled doughnuts almost in half. Spoon in pastry cream filling. Spread tops with frosting. Sprinkle with fleur de sel.

Makes about 12

AMARETTO CREAM DOUGHNUTS WITH VANILLA FROSTING AND SALTED ALMONDS

What is it about salty and sweet that is just so great? The amaretto liqueur and salted almonds raise this doughnut above the masses.

INGREDIENTS

For the filling
- ¾ cup (180ml) heavy cream
- Pinch salt
- ¼ cup (50g) superfine sugar
- ⅛ cup (20g) cornstarch
- 3 large egg yolks
- ¼ cup (60ml) amaretto liqueur (or use less liqueur and more cream)

For the doughnuts
- 2 tablespoons active dry yeast
- 1 cup (240ml) whole milk, warmed
- ½ cup (60g) white bread flour
- 3 cups (375g) all-purpose flour
- ¼ cup (60g) cold unsalted butter, grated
- 1 teaspoon vanilla extract
- 2 large eggs
- 1 large egg yolk

- 2 tablespoons plain yogurt
- ¼ cup (50g) superfine sugar
- ½ teaspoon salt

For the topping
- ½ cup (50g) slivered almonds
- 1 teaspoon olive oil
- Pinch salt
- Pinch sugar

For the frosting
- ¾ cup (75g) powdered sugar, sifted
- 2 tablespoons heavy cream
- ½ vanilla bean, split lengthwise, seeds scraped out

METHOD

Make the amaretto cream filling. Over medium heat, whisk together cream and salt and bring to a boil, stirring constantly. In a bowl, whisk sugar and cornstarch and beat in egg yolks. Slowly add egg mixture to the warm cream, whisking constantly. Continue to whisk for 2 minutes, or until the mixture thickens. Remove from heat and stir in liqueur. Let cool, press plastic wrap smoothly on the top to prevent a film, and chill.

In a large bowl, dissolve yeast in milk. Add bread flour and 1 ½ cups (190g) all-purpose flour. Mix in a stand mixer with paddle attachment until smooth. Cover and let rest for 20 minutes. Gradually add butter and mix until incorporated. Add vanilla, eggs, egg yolk, and yogurt. Turn off mixer, add sugar and salt, then mix on low until dough starts to come together.

With the dough hook, add the remaining flour in three stages. The dough should pull away from the sides of the bowl, but still be slightly sticky. If too wet, add a little flour. Cover and set in a warm place for 30 minutes. Gently press dough down and let sit for 1 hour, or until doubled.

Make the almond topping. Preheat oven to 350°F (175°C). Mix almonds, oil, salt, and sugar. Bake on a cookie sheet for 5 minutes. Let cool.

On a lightly floured surface, roll dough ½ inch (1.25cm) thick. Cut rounds with a 3 ½-inch (8.75cm) biscuit cutter, place on floured cookie sheets, cover with oiled plastic wrap, and let rise for 15 minutes.

Heat oil in a large, heavy pan to 360°F (182°C). Fry rounds for 3 minutes on first side, then 2 minutes on the other side, remove, and drain and cool on paper towels. Cut cooled doughnuts almost in half and fill with amaretto cream.

Make frosting. Whisk powdered sugar, cream, and vanilla seeds until smooth. Frost doughnut tops and sprinkle with the almond topping.

Makes about 12

RUM RAISIN CREAM DOUGHNUTS

This doughnut needs no other addition besides the rum raisin cream filling.
Just a slight sprinkle of powdered sugar and your stomach will applaud!

INGREDIENTS

For the filling
- ¾ cup (180ml) heavy cream
- Pinch salt
- ¼ cup (50g) superfine sugar
- ⅙ cup (20g) cornstarch
- 3 large egg yolks
- ¼ cup (60ml) dark rum (or use less rum and more cream)
- ¼ cup (30g) raisins
- Pinch ground cinnamon

For the doughnuts
- 2 tablespoons active dry yeast
- 1 cup (240ml) whole milk, warmed
- ½ cup (60g) white bread flour
- 3 cups (375g) all-purpose flour
- ¼ cup (60g) cold unsalted butter, grated
- 1 teaspoon vanilla extract
- 2 large eggs
- 1 large egg yolk
- 2 tablespoons plain yogurt
- ¼ cup (50g) superfine sugar
- ½ teaspoon salt
- Vegetable oil for deep-frying

For the decoration
- Powdered sugar for dusting

METHOD

Make the rum raisin cream filling. In a saucepan over medium heat, whisk together cream and salt and bring to a boil, stirring constantly. In a bowl, whisk sugar and cornstarch. Beat in egg yolks. Slowly add the egg mixture to the warm cream, whisking constantly. Continue to whisk for 2 minutes or until the mixture thickens. Remove from heat and stir in the rum, raisins, and cinnamon. Let cool, press plastic wrap smoothly on the top to prevent a film, and chill.

In a large bowl, dissolve yeast in milk. Add bread flour and 1 ½ cups (190g) all-purpose flour. Mix in a stand mixer with paddle attachment until smooth. Cover and let rest for 20 minutes. Gradually add butter and mix until incorporated. Add vanilla, eggs, egg yolk, and yogurt. Turn off mixer, add sugar and salt, then mix on low until dough starts to come together.

With the dough hook, add the remaining flour in three stages. The dough should pull away from the sides of the bowl nicely, but still be slightly sticky. If too wet, add a little flour. Cover and set in a warm place for 30 minutes. Gently press the dough down with your fist and let sit for 1 hour, or until doubled.

On a lightly floured surface, roll dough ½ inch (1.25cm) thick. Cut rounds with a 3 ½-inch (8.75cm) biscuit cutter (no hole in the center), place on floured cookie sheets, cover with oiled plastic wrap, and let rise for 15 minutes.

Heat oil in a large, heavy pan to 360°F (182°C). Fry doughnuts for 3 minutes on first side, then 2 minutes on the other side, remove, and drain on paper towels. Let cool, then cut almost in half. Spoon rum raisin cream inside. Place powdered sugar in a fine mesh strainer and dust the tops of the doughnuts before serving.

Makes about 12

PEACHES AND CREAM DOUGHNUTS

Ahhhhh...it's summer in the south! Warm peach filling inside a fluffy doughnut;
who could ask for anything more?

INGREDIENTS

For the filling
- ¾ cup (180ml) heavy cream
- Pinch salt
- ¼ cup (50g) superfine sugar
- ⅙ cup (20g) cornstarch
- 3 large egg yolks
- ¼ cup (60ml) peach schnapps
  (or use less and add more cream)
- 2–3 large ripe peaches, cut into sections,
  with skin

For the doughnuts
- 2 tablespoons active dry yeast
- 1 cup (240ml) whole milk, warmed
- ½ cup (60g) white bread flour
- 3 cups (375g) all-purpose flour
- ¼ cup (60g) cold unsalted butter, grated
- 1 teaspoon vanilla extract
- 2 large eggs
- 1 large egg yolk
- 2 tablespoons plain yogurt
- ¼ cup (50g) superfine sugar
- ½ teaspoon salt
- Vegetable oil for deep-frying

For the decoration
- Powdered sugar for dusting

METHOD

Make the peach cream filling. In a saucepan over medium heat, whisk together cream and salt and bring to a boil, stirring constantly. In a bowl, whisk sugar and cornstarch. Beat in egg yolks. Slowly add egg mixture to warm cream, whisking constantly to temper the eggs. Continue to whisk for 2 minutes, or until the mixture thickens. Remove from heat and stir in peach schnapps. Let cool, press plastic wrap smoothly on the top to prevent a film, and chill.

In a large bowl, dissolve yeast in milk. Add bread flour and 1 ½ cups (190g) all-purpose flour. Mix in a stand mixer with paddle attachment until smooth. Cover and let rest for 20 minutes. Gradually add butter and mix until incorporated. Add vanilla, eggs, egg yolk, and yogurt. Turn off mixer, add sugar and salt, then mix on low until dough starts to come together.

With the dough hook, add the remaining flour in three stages. The dough should pull away from the sides of the bowl nicely, but still be slightly sticky. If too wet, add a little flour. Cover and set in a warm place for 30 minutes. Gently press the dough down with your fist and let sit for 1 hour, or until doubled.

On a lightly floured surface, roll dough ½ inch (1.25cm) thick. Cut rounds with a 3 ½-inch (8.75cm) biscuit cutter (no hole in the center), place on floured cookie sheets, cover with oiled plastic wrap, and let rise for 15 minutes.

Heat oil in a large, heavy pan to 360°F (182°C). Fry doughnuts for 3 minutes on first side, then 2 minutes on the other side, remove, and drain on paper towels.

Once doughnuts have cooled, cut them almost in half. Spoon peach cream inside. Fan out peaches inside doughnuts. Place powdered sugar in a fine mesh strainer and dust the tops of the doughnuts.

Makes about 12

HAZELNUT CREAM DOUGHNUTS WITH NUTMEG GLAZE

More spicy than sweet, this doughnut goes well with some hot coffee and the morning paper.

INGREDIENTS

For the filling
- 1 cup (240ml) heavy cream
- Pinch salt
- ¼ cup (50g) superfine sugar
- ⅙ cup (20g) cornstarch
- 3 large egg yolks
- 1 teaspoon hazelnut flavoring
- ½ teaspoon vanilla extract

For the doughnuts
- 1 tablespoon active dry yeast
- 1 cup (240ml) whole milk, warmed
- ½ cup (60g) white bread flour
- 3 cups (375g) all-purpose flour
- ¼ cup (115g) cold unsalted butter, grated
- 1 teaspoon vanilla extract
- 2 large eggs
- 1 large egg yolk
- 2 tablespoons plain yogurt
- ¼ cup (50g) superfine sugar
- ½ teaspoon salt

For the glaze
- ¾ cup (75g) powdered sugar, sifted
- 2 tablespoons heavy cream
- 1 teaspoon ground nutmeg

METHOD

Make the hazelnut cream filling. In a saucepan over medium heat, whisk together cream and salt and bring to a boil, stirring constantly. In a separate bowl, whisk sugar and cornstarch. Beat in egg yolks. Slowly add the sugar and egg mixture to the warm cream, whisking constantly. Continue to whisk for 2 minutes or until the mixture thickens. Remove from heat and stir in flavorings. Let cool, press plastic wrap smoothly on the top to prevent a film, and chill.

In a large bowl, dissolve yeast in milk. Add bread flour and 1 ½ cups (190g) all-purpose flour. Mix in a stand mixer with paddle attachment until smooth. Cover and let rest for 20 minutes. Gradually add butter and mix until incorporated. Add vanilla, eggs, egg yolk, and yogurt. Turn off mixer, add sugar and salt, then mix on low until dough starts to come together.

With the dough hook, add the remaining flour in three stages. The dough should pull away from the sides of the bowl nicely, but still be slightly sticky. If too wet, add a little flour. Cover and set in a warm place for 30 minutes. Gently press dough down with your fist and let sit for 1 hour, or until doubled.

On a lightly floured surface, roll dough ½ inch (1.25cm) thick. Cut rounds using a 3 ½-inch (8.75cm) biscuit cutter (no hole in the center), place on floured cookie sheets, cover, and let rise for 15 minutes.

Heat the oil in a large, heavy pan to 360°F (182°C). Fry doughnuts for 3 minutes on first side, then 2 minutes on the other side, remove, and drain on paper towels. When cooled, cut almost in half and fill with hazelnut cream.

Make the glaze by whisking ingredients together. Drizzle glaze decoratively over doughnut tops. Let set before serving.

Makes about 12

Chapter 4

FAVORITE FLAVORS

There are some flavors, or combinations of flavors that are just so
evocative of childhood, like peanut butter and jelly, cookies and cream, or
butterscotch. Pair these flavors with doughnuts, and you have the kind of
experience that makes your taste buds soar.

SIMPLE GLAZED RING DOUGHNUTS

The purity of taste of a simple doughnut ring, topped with a vanilla or chocolate glaze, just cannot be beaten.

INGREDIENTS

For the doughnuts
- ¾ cup (180ml) whole milk, warmed
- ¼ cup (50g) superfine sugar
- 1 package (2 ¼ teaspoons) active dry yeast
- 2 ½ cups (250g) all-purpose flour
- ¼ teaspoon salt
- 2 large egg yolks
- 2 tablespoons (30g) unsalted butter, room temperature
- Vegetable oil for deep-frying

- **For the glaze**
- ¼ cup (60ml) whole milk
- 1 teaspoon vanilla extract
- 1 ½ cups (150g) powdered sugar, sifted

METHOD

Line two large cookie sheets with parchment paper.

Place the milk in a small bowl, stir in the sugar and yeast, and leave for 10–15 minutes.

With a dough hook in the bowl of a stand mixer, mix together the flour and the salt. Make a well in the center and add the egg yolks, butter, and yeast liquid. Mix with the machine on medium speed for about 3–4 minutes until a dough forms and comes away from the sides of the bowl. Mix for 2–3 more minutes. The dough should be slightly sticky. If it is too wet, add more flour; too dry, add more milk. Transfer to a large lightly oiled bowl, cover, and leave for an hour.

Transfer dough to a lightly floured work surface, punch down, and roll out to a thickness of ⅜ inch (1cm). Cut out about 14 doughnuts, using a 3 ½-inch (8.75cm) doughnut cutter, and place them, and the holes, an inch (2.5cm) apart on the cookie sheets. Cover with oiled plastic wrap and leave for an hour.

Heat the oil in a heavy, large pan to 360°F (182°C). Fry the doughnuts for 2 minutes on each side, and the doughnut holes for 1 minute on the first side, ½ minute on the second. Drain on paper towels, then cool on a wire rack.

Make the glaze. In a small pan over a gentle heat, warm the milk and vanilla together, and gradually add the sifted powdered sugar until you get a slightly runny consistency for dipping.

Dip top of each doughnut and doughnut hole in the glaze, and return to the wire rack to set. Serve immediately.

Makes 14 doughnuts and 14 doughnut holes

TIP
For an alternative topping, make a delicious chocolate glaze. Melt 2 tablespoons semisweet chocolate chips in the pan with the milk and vanilla, and add the sugar as before.

JELLY DOUGHNUTS

Filled with strawberry jelly and rolled in sugar, these doughnuts are wonderful for breakfast with steaming hot coffee or creamy hot chocolate.

INGREDIENTS

For the doughnuts
- ⅔ cup (160ml) whole milk, warmed
- 1 package (2 ¼ teaspoons) active dry yeast
- 3 ¾ cups (470g) all-purpose flour
- 1 teaspoon salt
- ½ cup (100g) superfine sugar
- 2 large eggs, room temperature, lightly beaten
- 1 teaspoon vanilla extract
- ½ cup (115g) salted butter, room temperature, cut into small pieces
- Vegetable oil for deep-frying

For the filling and decoration
- ½ cup (170g) strawberry (or your favorite) jelly
- 1 cup (200g) superfine sugar

METHOD

Line two large cookie sheets with parchment paper.

In the bowl of a stand mixer fitted with a dough hook, stir the milk and yeast together. Leave for 5 minutes. Add the flour, salt, sugar, eggs, and vanilla, and mix on low speed for 3–4 minutes until the dough begins to come together. Add the butter a piece at a time, continuing to mix on a low speed, until all the butter has been incorporated. The dough should be quite sticky, but not overly so. Transfer the dough to a large, lightly oiled bowl, cover, and chill in the refrigerator for 6–15 hours.

Turn the dough out onto a lightly floured work surface, and punch down. Divide the dough into 15 equal pieces and flatten out each piece slightly. Spoon a teaspoon of strawberry jelly into the middle of each piece and fold up the dough around the filling, pinching well to seal it. Place an inch (2.5cm) apart on the cookie sheets, seam underneath. Cover with oiled plastic wrap and leave for an hour.

Place ½ cup (100g) superfine sugar in a wide shallow bowl and set aside.

Heat the oil in a heavy, large pan to 360°F (182°C). Fry the doughnuts for 3 minutes on the first side, 2 minutes on the second, then drain on paper towels. Roll each doughnut in the sugar to coat all over. Either serve warm or completely cooled.

Makes 15

GLUTEN- AND DAIRY-FREE DOUGHNUTS

Even if you cannot eat wheat, gluten, or dairy products, you can still enjoy
a delicious glazed doughnut for breakfast.

INGREDIENTS

For the doughnuts
- ½ cup (60g) white rice flour
- ⅓ cup (40g) tapioca flour
- ⅓ cup (40g) potato starch
- 1 teaspoon baking powder
- ½ teaspoon baking soda
- ½ teaspoon salt
- ¾ teaspoon xanthan gum or CMC powder
- ¾ cup (150g) superfine sugar
- 1 large egg, room temperature, lightly beaten
- ½ cup (120ml) rice milk
- Juice of 1 lemon
- 1 tablespoon vegetable oil

For the glaze
- 1 cup (100g) powdered sugar, sifted
- 2–3 tablespoons water
- ½ teaspoon glycerine (optional)

METHOD

Preheat the oven to 350°F (175°C) and spray two 6-cup doughnut pans with oil.

In a medium bowl, whisk together the rice and tapioca flours, potato starch, baking powder, baking soda, salt, xanthan gum, and sugar. In a separate bowl, whisk together the egg, rice milk, lemon juice, and vegetable oil. Pour the egg mixture into the flour mixture and mix until blended.

Spoon or pipe the mixture into the doughnut pans, filling them two-thirds full. Bake for 10–12 minutes, or until a toothpick inserted into the center comes out clean. Let doughnuts cool in the pans for 5 minutes, then transfer to a wire rack to cool completely.

While the doughnuts are cooling, make the glaze. In a bowl, mix the powdered sugar and add enough water to make a slightly runny glaze. Add the glycerine, if using, which will keep the glaze soft. Dip the tops of the cooled doughnuts in the glaze and place back on the wire rack to set.

Makes 11–12

HOT CROSS DOUGHNUTS

Lightly spiced, filled with juicy raisins and sweet raspberry preserves, these doughnuts will make a great addition to your breakfast repertoire.

INGREDIENTS

For the doughnuts
- ⅔ cup (160ml) whole milk, warmed
- 1 package (2 ¼ teaspoons) active dry yeast
- 3 ¾ cups (470g) all-purpose flour
- 1 teaspoon ground cinnamon
- ½ teaspoon ground nutmeg
- ½ teaspoon ground ginger
- 1 teaspoon salt
- ½ cup (100g) superfine sugar
- 2 large eggs, room temperature, lightly beaten
- ½ cup (115g) salted butter, room temperature, cut into small pieces
- ½ cup (60g) raisins
- Vegetable oil for deep-frying

For the filling
- ½ cup (170g) raspberry preserves

For the decoration
- 2 tablespoons flour
- 4–5 tablespoons water
- 1 cup (200g) superfine sugar

METHOD

Line two large cookie sheets with parchment paper.

With a dough hook in the bowl of a stand mixer, stir the milk and yeast together. Leave for 5 minutes. Add the flour, spices, salt, sugar, and eggs, and mix on low speed for 3–4 minutes until the dough begins to come together. Add the butter a piece at a time, continuing to mix on a low speed, until all the butter has been incorporated. The dough should be quite sticky, but not overly so. Add the raisins and mix until they are evenly distributed through the dough. Place the dough in a large, lightly oiled bowl, cover, and chill in the refrigerator for 6–15 hours.

Turn the dough out onto a lightly floured work surface and punch down. Divide the dough into 15 equal pieces and flatten out each piece slightly. Spoon a generous teaspoon of raspberry preserves into the middle of each piece and fold up the dough around the filling, pinching well to seal it. Place an inch (2.5cm) apart on the cookie sheets, seam underneath.

Make the cross for decoration by mixing the flour with the water in a small bowl. Using a pastry bag or a plastic bag with the corner cut off, pipe a line one way across all the doughnuts. Turn the cookie sheet 90 degrees and pipe another line across the tops to make a cross. Spray the tops lightly with a little oil and leave for an hour. Place 1 cup (200g) superfine sugar in a wide shallow bowl and set aside.

Heat the oil in a heavy, large pan to 360°F (182°C). Fry the doughnuts for 3 minutes on the first side, 2 minutes on the second. Drain on paper towels, then roll in the sugar to coat all over. Serve warm or cooled completely.

Makes 15

TIP
Make a Christmas alternative by omitting the cross on the top and adding candied cherries and chopped almonds and wrapping the dough around a marzipan center to make baby stollen.

BUTTERSCOTCH AND MAPLE YUM-YUM TWISTS

These yeast-raised doughnuts are rolled out like puff pastry dough, which makes them flakier. Smothered with butterscotch and maple frosting, and scattered with pecans, they are fit for a king.

INGREDIENTS

For the twists
- ⅔ cup (160ml) whole milk, warmed
- 1 package (2 ¼ teaspoons) active dry yeast
- 3 ¾ cups (470g) all-purpose flour
- 1 teaspoon salt
- ½ cup (100g) superfine sugar
- 2 large eggs, room temperature, lightly beaten
- ½ cup (115g) salted butter, room temperature, cut into small pieces
- 1 teaspoon vanilla extract
- Vegetable oil for deep-frying

For the coating
- 1 cup (200g) superfine sugar

For the frosting
- ⅓ cup (75g) salted butter
- 1 cup (200g) brown sugar
- ¼ cup (60ml) heavy cream
- 1 cup (100g) powdered sugar, sifted, plus more if needed
- 1 tablespoon maple syrup
- 1 teaspoon vanilla extract

For the decoration
- ⅓ cup (40g) chopped pecans

METHOD

Line two large cookie sheets with parchment paper.

With a dough hook in the bowl of a stand mixer, stir the milk and yeast together. Leave for 5 minutes. Add the flour, salt, sugar, and eggs, and mix on low speed for 3–4 minutes until the dough begins to come together. Add the butter a piece at a time. Add the vanilla. The dough should be slightly sticky. If it is too wet, add more flour; too dry, add more milk. Transfer to a large, lightly oiled bowl, cover, and chill in the refrigerator for 6–15 hours.

Transfer the dough to a lightly floured work surface, punch down, and divide into three equal pieces. Roll out one piece into a 12 x 6-inch (30.5 x 15.25cm) rectangle. Cut into strips to make four 6 x 3-inch (15.25 x 7.5cm) pieces. Cut each strip in half lengthwise and roll one half slightly longer than the other. You will end up with eight strips, four of which are slightly longer. Wrap one longer piece around one shorter piece two or three times and match up the ends, sealing them well. Place an inch (2.5cm) apart on the parchment-lined cookie sheets. Repeat with the other two rectangles, making 12. Cover with oiled plastic wrap and leave for an hour.

Put 1 cup (200g) superfine sugar in a shallow bowl. Heat the oil in a heavy, large pan to 360°F (182°C). Fry the twists for 3 minutes on each side, drain on paper towels, and roll in the sugar. Cool on a wire rack.

Make the frosting. In a small pan, melt the butter and brown sugar. Bring to a boil, simmer for 2 minutes, add cream, stir for 2 minutes, remove from the heat, and cool for 5 minutes. Stir in the powdered sugar, maple syrup, vanilla, and more cream if necessary to make a pouring consistency. Pour over the twists and scatter with a few pecans. Return to the wire rack to set.

Makes 12

PEANUT BUTTER AND JELLY DOUGHNUTS WITH PEANUT BUTTER FROSTING

Hidden inside these doughnuts is the classic combination of peanut butter and jelly, topped with a creamy peanut butter frosting.

INGREDIENTS

For the doughnuts
- ⅓ cup (80ml) warm water
- 1 teaspoon superfine sugar
- 1 package (2 ¼ teaspoons) active dry yeast
- 3 cups (375g) all-purpose flour
- ¾ cup (90g) white bread flour
- ½ cup (100g) superfine sugar
- 2 teaspoons salt
- ⅓ cup (80ml) whole milk, warmed
- 2 large eggs, room temperature, lightly beaten
- ½ cup (115g) salted butter, room temperature, cut into small pieces
- Vegetable oil for deep-frying

For the filling
- ¼ cup (85g) strawberry jelly
- ¼ cup (65g) smooth or crunchy peanut butter

For the frosting
- 1 tablespoon whole milk
- ½ cup (160g) milk chocolate chips
- 2 tablespoons smooth peanut butter
- ¾ cup (75g) powdered sugar, sifted

METHOD

Line two large cookie sheets with parchment paper.

Place the warm water in a medium bowl, stir in the teaspoon of sugar and the yeast, and leave for 10–15 minutes.

With the dough hook in the bowl of a stand mixer, stir both flours, ½ cup (100g) superfine sugar, and salt together. Add the yeast liquid, warm milk, and beaten eggs, and mix until the dough comes together. On medium speed, add the pieces of butter, ensuring each piece is fully incorporated before you add the next piece, about 5–7 minutes. The dough should be slightly sticky. If it is too wet, add more flour; too dry, add more water. Transfer to a lightly oiled bowl, cover, and leave for an hour until doubled.

Transfer the dough to a lightly floured work surface, knead twice, divide into 15 equal pieces, and flatten out each piece. Spoon a teaspoon of strawberry jelly and a teaspoon of peanut butter into the middle of each piece and fold up the dough around the filling, sealing well. Place an inch (2.5cm) apart on the cookie sheets, seam underneath, cover with oiled plastic wrap, and leave for 30 minutes.

Heat the oil in a heavy, large pan to 360°F (182°C). Fry the doughnuts for 3 minutes on the first side, 2 minutes on the second. Drain on paper towels and cool on a wire rack.

Make the peanut butter frosting. In a small pan over a gentle heat, warm the milk, chocolate chips, and peanut butter together, stirring until melted. Add the sifted powdered sugar, a little at a time, stirring until it is smooth. Let cool. Swirl frosting on top of the cooled doughnuts.

Makes 15

COOKIES AND CREAM DOUGHNUTS

These are first glazed with a soft frosting, before being decorated with chopped chocolate cookies and finished with a rich cream and chocolate cookie mix swirled on the top.

INGREDIENTS

For the doughnuts
- 1 cup (125g) all-purpose flour
- 2 tablespoons unsweetened cocoa powder, sifted
- 1 teaspoon baking powder
- ¼ teaspoon baking soda
- ½ teaspoon ground cinnamon
- ½ teaspoon salt
- 1 ounce (30g) semisweet chocolate, grated
- 2 tablespoons semisweet chocolate chips
- ½ cup (100g) superfine sugar
- ¼ cup (60ml) plus 2 tablespoons buttermilk
- ¼ cup (60ml) whole milk
- 1 large egg, room temperature, lightly beaten
- ½ teaspoon vanilla extract

For the glaze
- 1 cup (100g) powdered sugar, sifted
- 2–3 tablespoons whole milk
- ½ teaspoon glycerine (optional)

For the decoration
- 8 chocolate cream cookies, chopped
- 1 cup (240ml) heavy cream
- 2 chocolate cream-filled cookies, finely crushed

METHOD

Spray two 6-cup doughnut pans with oil and preheat the oven to 325°F (160°F).

In a medium bowl, whisk together the flour, cocoa powder, baking powder, baking soda, cinnamon, and salt. Add the grated chocolate, chocolate chips, and sugar, and stir to combine.

In a separate bowl, whisk together the buttermilk, milk, egg, and vanilla. Pour into the flour mixture, and stir to combine. Spoon or pipe the mixture into the doughnut cups, filling them two-thirds full. Bake for 10 minutes, or until a toothpick inserted into the center comes out clean. Let cool in the pans for 5 minutes, then transfer to a wire rack to cool completely.

Make the glaze. In a bowl, place the powdered sugar and add enough milk to make a thick glaze. Add the glycerine, if using, which will keep the glaze soft. Dip the top of each doughnut in the glaze and place back on the wire rack to set.

Place the chopped cookies around the top of the doughnuts decoratively. In a medium bowl, whip the cream to soft peaks and fold in the crushed cookies. Using a large piping tip, pipe a generous decorative swirl in the middle of each doughnut before serving.

Makes 10

PEANUT BUTTER CUP DOUGHNUTS

These peanut butter doughnuts are baked and topped with chocolate and peanut butter cups and finished with a flourish of peanut butter, swirled into the center.

INGREDIENTS

For the doughnuts
- ¼ cup (65g) smooth peanut butter
- ¼ cup (50g) superfine sugar
- ⅓ cup (80ml) plus 1 tablespoon whole milk
- 1 tablespoon vegetable oil
- 1 large egg, room temperature, lightly beaten
- 1 teaspoon vanilla extract
- 1 cup (125g) all-purpose flour
- 1 teaspoon baking powder
- ½ teaspoon salt
- ½ teaspoon ground cinnamon

For the frosting
- ¼ cup (60g) unsalted butter
- 2 tablespoons whole milk
- 2 teaspoons light corn syrup
- 1 teaspoon vanilla extract
- ⅓ cup (100g) semisweet chocolate chips
- 1 cup (100g) powdered sugar, sifted

For the decoration
- ⅓ cup (85g) smooth peanut butter
- 3 tablespoons powdered sugar, sifted
- 1 tablespoon (15g) unsalted butter, room temperature
- 3 tablespoons chopped mini peanut butter cups

METHOD

Preheat the oven to 325°F (160°F) and spray a 6-cup doughnut pan with oil.

Using an electric mixer, whisk together the peanut butter and sugar until fluffy. Add milk, oil, egg, and vanilla extract, and continue to mix until combined. Add the flour, baking powder, salt, and cinnamon, and mix until smooth. Spoon or pipe the batter into the doughnut pan, filling the cups two-thirds full. Bake in the preheated oven for 8–10 minutes, or until a toothpick inserted into the center comes out clean. Cool in the pan for 5 minutes before turning out onto a wire rack to cool.

Make the frosting. In a small pan, melt the butter with the milk, corn syrup, and vanilla extract. Add the chocolate chips and stir until melted and smooth. Add the powdered sugar a little at a time, stirring until smooth. Remove from the heat. Dip the tops of the doughnuts into the frosting and place back on the wire rack to cool and set.

In a small bowl, mix the peanut butter with the powdered sugar and butter until smooth, and pipe a little swirl into the middle of each doughnut. Decorate with chopped mini peanut butter cups and serve.

Makes 6

PUMPKIN DOUGHNUTS WITH GINGERBREAD GLAZE

Warm pumpkin and spicy gingerbread remind me of my childhood when I would sneak a taste of pumpkin pie. You won't have to sneak these, unless you don't want to share!

INGREDIENTS

For the doughnuts
- 1 ¾ cups (220g) all-purpose flour
- 2 teaspoons baking powder
- ¼ teaspoon baking soda
- ½ teaspoon salt
- ½ teaspoon ground cinnamon
- ¼ teaspoon ground ginger
- ⅛ teaspoon ground nutmeg
- Pinch ground cloves
- 1 ½ tablespoons (25g) cold unsalted butter, grated
- ½ cup (100g) superfine sugar
- 1 large egg
- 1 large egg yolk
- ½ teaspoon vanilla extract
- ¼ cup (60ml) plus ½ tablespoon buttermilk
- ½ cup (120g) canned pumpkin purée
- Vegetable oil for deep-frying

For the glaze
- ¾ cup (75g) powdered sugar, sifted
- 3 tablespoons heavy cream
- 1 tablespoon dark molasses
- ¼ teaspoon ground cinnamon
- ⅛ teaspoon ground ginger
- ⅛ teaspoon ground nutmeg
- ½ teaspoon vanilla extract

For the decoration (optional)
- ½ cup (70g) crushed graham crackers

METHOD

Whisk the flour, baking powder, baking soda, salt, and spices in a medium bowl to blend.

In the bowl of a stand mixer, cream the butter and sugar until blended. Beat in the egg, then the egg yolk and vanilla. Gradually beat in the buttermilk. Beat in the pumpkin purée in four additions. Using a rubber spatula, fold in the dry ingredients in four additions, blending gently after each addition. Cover the bowl with plastic wrap and chill for 3 hours.

Remove the dough from the refrigerator and roll out ½ inch (1.25cm) thick. Cut dough with a 3 ½-inch (8.75cm) doughnut cutter. Put doughnuts about an inch (2.5cm) apart on floured cookie sheets and cover with oiled plastic wrap. Put the pans back in the refrigerator for 20 minutes.

Heat the oil in a large, heavy pan to 360°F (182°C). Gently place a few doughnuts in the pan at a time. Fry for 2 minutes per side, then remove with a slotted spoon and place on paper towels.

Make the glaze. In a medium bowl, whisk all the glaze ingredients together until desired consistency. Dip the tops of doughnuts in the glaze and place on paper towels. Before the glaze fully sets, sprinkle crushed graham crackers on top if desired.

Makes about 15

BURNED CARAMEL DOUGHNUTS WITH SEA SALT

The complex flavors in this doughnut will awaken your taste buds! Burned caramel has a wonderfully rich flavor and the flaky fleur de sel melts in your mouth.

INGREDIENTS

For the doughnuts
- 2 tablespoons active dry yeast
- 1 cup (240ml) whole milk, warmed
- ½ cup (60g) white bread flour
- 3 cups (375g) all-purpose flour
- ¼ cup (60g) cold unsalted butter, grated
- 1 teaspoon vanilla extract
- 2 large eggs
- 1 large egg yolk
- 2 tablespoons plain yogurt
- ¼ cup (50g) superfine sugar
- ½ teaspoon salt
- Vegetable oil for deep-frying

For the glaze
- 3 tablespoons (45g) unsalted butter
- ½ cup (100g) superfine sugar
- ¼ cup (60ml) heavy cream

For the decoration
- Fleur de sel (or plain sea salt) for sprinkling

METHOD

In a large mixing bowl, dissolve yeast in milk. Add the bread flour and 1 ½ cups (190g) all-purpose flour. Mix in a stand mixer with the paddle attachment until smooth. Cover and let rest for 20 minutes. Gradually add the butter and mix until incorporated. Add the vanilla, eggs, egg yolk, and yogurt. Turn off mixer, add the sugar and salt, then mix on low until the dough starts to come together.

With the dough hook attachment, add the remaining flour in three stages. The dough should pull away from the sides of the bowl, but still be slightly sticky. If too wet, add a little more flour. Cover and set in a warm place for 30 minutes. Gently press dough down with your fist and let sit again for 1 hour, or until the dough has doubled.

On a lightly floured surface, roll dough ½ inch (1.25cm) thick. Cut rounds with a 3 ½-inch (8.75cm) doughnut cutter, place on floured cookie sheets, cover with oiled plastic wrap, and let rise for 15 minutes.

Heat the oil in a large, heavy pan to 360°F (182°C). Fry a few doughnuts at a time for 2 minutes on each side, then remove with a slotted spoon and place on paper towels to drain and cool.

Make the caramel glaze. In a small saucepan over medium heat, let the butter cook until it turns golden brown. Remove from heat. In a separate pan, cook the sugar over medium heat until it smells smoky and turns a warm brown color, whisking continuously to brown evenly. Remove from heat and add the butter. Slowly whisk in cream. Set aside to cool.

Dip the doughnut tops in the caramel glaze, and place on paper towels to set. While the glaze is still sticky, sprinkle with fleur de sel.

Makes about 12

VANILLA-FROSTED DOUGHNUTS

Why mess with a classic? Caution: this doughnut will bring about nostalgia!

INGREDIENTS

For the doughnuts
- 2 tablespoons active dry yeast
- 1 cup (240ml) whole milk, warmed
- ½ cup (60g) white bread flour
- 3 cups (375g) all-purpose flour
- ¼ cup (60g) cold unsalted butter, grated
- 1 teaspoon vanilla extract
- 2 large eggs
- 1 large egg yolk
- 2 tablespoons plain yogurt
- ¼ cup (50g) superfine sugar
- ½ teaspoon salt
- Vegetable oil for deep-frying

For the glaze
- 1 cup (100g) powdered sugar, sifted
- 3 tablespoons heavy cream
- ½ teaspoon vanilla extract
- ½ vanilla bean, split lengthwise, seeds scraped out

METHOD

In a large mixing bowl, dissolve yeast in milk. Add the bread flour and 1 ½ cups (190g) all-purpose flour. Mix in a stand mixer with the paddle attachment until smooth. Cover and let rest for 20 minutes. Gradually add the butter and mix until incorporated. Add the vanilla, eggs, egg yolk, and yogurt. Turn off mixer, add the sugar and salt, then mix on low until the dough starts to come together.

With the dough hook attachment, add the remaining flour in three stages. The dough should pull away from the sides of the bowl nicely, but still be slightly sticky. If too wet, add a little flour. Cover and set in a warm place for 30 minutes. Gently press the dough down with your fist and let sit again for 1 hour, or until the dough has doubled.

Turn dough out onto a lightly floured surface and roll ½ inch (1.25cm) thick. Cut rounds using a 3 ½-inch (8.75cm) doughnut cutter, place on floured cookie sheets, cover with oiled plastic wrap, and let rise for 15 minutes.

Heat the oil in a large, heavy pan to 360°F (182°C). Gently place a few doughnuts in the pan at a time. Fry for 2 minutes per side, then remove with a slotted spoon and place on paper towels.

Make the glaze. In a small bowl, whisk together powdered sugar, cream, vanilla extract, and vanilla seeds to a smooth consistency. Dunk doughnut tops in the glaze and set on paper towels to dry.

Makes about 12

VEGAN LEMON-LAVENDER GLAZED DOUGHNUTS

Fresh-squeezed lemon adds the most amazing tartness to this summer-style doughnut. Lavender balances the tartness with a wonderful floral twist. And they're vegan! Lavender seeds can be found in your local health food store or online.

INGREDIENTS

For the doughnuts
- 1 ¼ tablespoons cornstarch
- 1 ¼ tablespoons potato starch
- Heaping ¼ teaspoon baking powder
- ½ cup (60ml) water
- 1 teaspoon vegetable oil
- 2 tablespoons active dry yeast
- 1 cup (240ml) soy milk, warmed (or use any dairy alternative)
- ½ cup (60g) white bread flour
- 3 cups (375g) all-purpose flour
- ¼ cup (50g) vegetable shortening
- ½ tablespoon vanilla extract
- ¼ cup (50g) superfine sugar
- ½ teaspoon salt
- ½ tablespoon freshly grated lemon zest
- Vegetable oil for deep-frying

For the glaze
- 2 tablespoons lemon juice
- 3 tablespoons lavender seeds
- 1 cup (100g) powdered sugar, sifted

METHOD

Whisk together the cornstarch, potato starch, and baking powder. Whisk in water and oil and incorporate fully. This is the egg replacer.

In a mixing bowl, dissolve yeast in soy milk. Add the bread flour and 1 ½ cups (190g) all-purpose flour. Mix in a stand mixer with the paddle attachment until smooth. Cover and let rest for 20 minutes. Mix in shortening, then the vanilla and egg replacer. Turn off mixer; add sugar, salt, and lemon zest; then mix on low until the dough starts to come together.

Using the dough hook, add the remaining flour in three stages. The dough should pull away from the sides of the bowl, but still be sticky. If too sticky, add more flour; if too dry, add more milk. Cover and set in a warm place for 30 minutes. Gently press dough down with your fist and rest again for 1 hour, or until doubled.

On a lightly floured surface, roll dough ½ inch (1.25cm) thick. Cut rounds with a 3 ½-inch (8.75cm) biscuit cutter (no hole in center). Heat the oil in a heavy, large pan to 360°F (182°C), gently add a few rounds, and fry for 3 minutes on the first side, 2 minutes on the second side. When they are golden brown, remove with a slotted spoon and let drain on paper towels. Cool on cooling racks.

Make the glaze. In a small saucepan over medium heat, combine the lemon juice and lavender seeds. Bring to a low boil, remove from the heat to cool, then whisk in the powdered sugar to desired consistency. Dip doughnut tops in the glaze and place on paper towels to set.

Makes about 12

CHAI DOUGHNUTS

This doughnut tastes so close to a nice hot cup of chai, you won't believe it! The spiciness pairs well with a tall glass of coconut water.

INGREDIENTS

For the doughnuts
- 2 tablespoons active dry yeast
- 1 cup (240ml) whole milk, warmed
- ½ cup (60g) white bread flour
- 3 cups (375g) all-purpose flour
- ¼ cup (60g) cold unsalted butter, grated
- 1 teaspoon vanilla extract
- 2 large eggs
- 1 large egg yolk
- 2 tablespoons plain yogurt
- ¼ cup (50g) superfine sugar
- ½ teaspoon salt
- Vegetable oil for deep-frying

For the glaze
- 1 cup (100g) powdered sugar, sifted
- 3 tablespoons heavy cream
- 1 teaspoon ground cinnamon
- 1 teaspoon ground nutmeg
- ½ teaspoon ground cloves
- Pinch ground cardamom

METHOD

In a large mixing bowl, dissolve yeast in milk. Add the bread flour and 1 ½ cups (190g) all-purpose flour. Mix in a stand mixer with the paddle attachment until smooth. Cover and let rest for 20 minutes. Gradually add the butter and mix until incorporated. Add the vanilla, eggs, egg yolk, and yogurt. Turn off mixer, add the sugar and salt, then mix on low until the dough starts to come together.

With the dough hook attachment, add the remaining flour in three stages. The dough should pull away from the sides of the bowl nicely, but still be slightly sticky. If too wet, add a little flour. Cover and set in a warm place for 30 minutes. Gently press the dough down with your fist and let sit again for 1 hour, or until the dough has doubled.

Turn the dough out onto a lightly floured surface and roll ½ inch (1.25cm) thick. Cut rounds using a 3 ½-inch (8.75cm) doughnut cutter, place on floured cookie sheets, cover with oiled plastic wrap, and let rise for 15 minutes.

Heat the oil in a large, heavy pan to 360°F (182°C). Fry a few doughnuts at a time for 2 minutes per side, then remove with a slotted spoon and place on paper towels to drain.

Make the glaze. In a small bowl, whisk together the powdered sugar, cream, and spices to a smooth consistency. Dunk the doughnut tops in the glaze and place on paper towels to set.

Makes about 12

RED VELVET DOUGHNUTS

Love chocolate but bored with chocolate cake? These are so yummy, you'll want to eat all of them!
Perfect for your sweetie on Valentine's Day.

INGREDIENTS

For the doughnuts
- 3 cups (375g) all-purpose flour
- 1 ⅛ cups (100g) unsweetened cocoa powder
- 2 cups (400g) superfine sugar
- 2 teaspoons baking soda
- Pinch salt
- ¾ cup (180ml) vegetable oil
- 2 cups (475ml) cold water
- 2 teaspoons vanilla extract
- 2 tablespoons white vinegar
- 1 tablespoon red food coloring

For the frosting
- 4 ounces (115g) cream cheese, room temperature
- 1 cup (100g) powdered sugar, sifted
- 2 tablespoons (30g) cold unsalted butter, grated
- ½ teaspoon vanilla extract

For the decoration (optional)
- Chopped walnuts

METHOD

Preheat the oven to 350°F (175°C). Spray two 12-cup doughnut pans with oil. In the bowl of a stand mixer, combine the flour, cocoa, sugar, baking soda, and salt. Add the oil, water, vanilla, vinegar, and food coloring. Mix until smooth. The batter will be thin.

Fill doughnut cups three-quarters full with batter. Bake for 10–12 minutes, or until a toothpick inserted in the center comes out clean. Allow to cool for 5 minutes in the pans, then remove and let cool on cooling racks.

In the bowl of a stand mixer, place all the ingredients for the cream cheese frosting. Mix on medium speed until the frosting is smooth and spreadable. Spread the tops of the doughnuts with an ample amount of the frosting. Sprinkle chopped walnuts on top, if desired.

Makes 24

Chapter 5

RICH & CHOCOLATEY

What's better than chocolate? Lots and lots of chocolate! Tantalize your
taste buds with a Spicy Hot Chocolate Doughnut or a decadent Truffle
Cake Ball. Whether you're a chocoholic or just a chocolate enthusiast, this
chapter will fulfill all of your cacao dreams.

TRUFFLE CAKE BALLS

It is not often that we find ourselves with leftover doughnuts, but if we do, forming them into balls and covering them in chocolate is a great way to use them up. Either yeast-raised or cake doughnuts will work fine.

INGREDIENTS

- 2 cups (300g) stale vanilla or chocolate doughnut crumbs
- 3–4 tablespoons cold strong espresso coffee or your favorite liqueur
- 6 ounces (170g) semisweet or milk chocolate, plus extra for decoration if desired

METHOD

Line a large cookie sheet with parchment paper.

Place the crumbs in a medium bowl and add about 3 tablespoons cold espresso or liqueur. Form the mixture into balls about 1 inch (2.5cm) in size, adding extra liquid if necessary. Place the balls on the cookie sheet, cover, and chill in the refrigerator for 30 minutes.

In a bowl set over a pan of barely simmering water, melt the chocolate. Using two forks, quickly dip one ball at a time in the chocolate, turning it to coat it all over, and then removing it to drain and set on the parchment paper. Repeat with all the truffle balls. If desired, drizzle a little darker or lighter chocolate back and forth over each chocolate-covered ball to decorate.

Makes 10

TIP
This recipe works very well at holiday times using a liqueur such as Grand Marnier or cherry brandy in place of espresso.

BAKED CHOCOLATE DOUGHNUTS WITH MINTY GLAZE

Chocolate doughnuts flavored with a minty glaze and decorated with chocolate sprinkles are wonderful, especially for holidays.

INGREDIENTS

For the doughnuts
- 1 ¾ cups (220g) all-purpose flour
- ¾ cup (150g) superfine sugar
- 3 tablespoons unsweetened cocoa powder, sifted
- 2 teaspoons baking powder
- 1 teaspoon ground cinnamon
- 1 teaspoon salt
- 2 ounces (60g) mint or semisweet chocolate, grated
- ¾ cup (180ml) whole milk
- 2 large eggs, room temperature, lightly beaten
- 2 tablespoons (30g) salted butter, softened
- 1 teaspoon instant coffee powder
- 1 teaspoon vanilla extract
- ¼ cup (80g) semisweet chocolate chips

For the glaze
- 1 cup (100g) powdered sugar, sifted
- 2–3 tablespoons whole milk
- Drop peppermint extract
- Tiny drop green food coloring (optional)
- ½ teaspoon glycerine (optional)

For the decoration
- ¼ cup (40g) chocolate sprinkles

METHOD

Preheat the oven to 325°F (160°F) and spray two 6-cup doughnut pans with oil.

In a large bowl, whisk together the flour, sugar, cocoa powder, baking powder, cinnamon, and salt. Add the grated chocolate and stir to blend. In a separate bowl, whisk together the milk, eggs, softened butter, instant coffee powder, and vanilla extract. Pour into the flour mixture, add the chocolate chips, and stir to combine.

Using a pastry bag (a disposable one is great for this, or use a zippered plastic bag with the corner cut off), fill the doughnut pans three-quarters full. Bake in the preheated oven for about 10 minutes, or until a toothpick inserted in the center comes out clean. Let the doughnuts cool in the pans for 5 minutes, then carefully transfer to a wire rack to cool.

Make the glaze. In a bowl, place the powdered sugar and add enough milk to make a thick glaze. Add the peppermint extract, and if using, the green food coloring and glycerine (to keep the glaze soft). Dip the top of each doughnut in the glaze and return to the wire rack to set. Decorate with chocolate sprinkles.

Makes 16

GLUTEN-FREE CHOCOLATE-ORANGE DOUGHNUTS

Orange zest gives these doughnuts a delicious tang and the banana keeps them moist.

INGREDIENTS

For the doughnuts
- ½ cup (60g) rice flour
- ⅓ cup (40g) potato starch
- ⅙ cup (20g) tapioca flour
- ½ cup (100g) superfine sugar
- 1 teaspoon baking powder
- 1 teaspoon xanthan gum or CMC powder
- 1 teaspoon ground cinnamon
- ¼ teaspoon salt
- 2 tablespoons semisweet chocolate chips
- Grated zest of 1 large orange
- ¼ cup (60g) salted butter, melted
- 1 large egg, room temperature
- 2 tablespoons buttermilk
- 1 large ripe banana, mashed

For the glaze
- 4 ounces (115g) semisweet or orange-flavored chocolate, melted

For the decoration
- 1 tablespoon sugar sprinkles

METHOD

Preheat the oven to 350°F (175°C) and spray a 6-cup doughnut pan with oil.

In a large bowl, whisk together the rice flour, potato starch, tapioca flour, sugar, baking powder, xanthan gum, cinnamon, and salt. Stir in the chocolate chips and orange zest. Make a well in the center and add the melted butter, beaten egg, buttermilk, and mashed banana. Mix well until combined.

Pipe or spoon the batter into the prepared doughnut pan. Bake for 12 minutes, leave in the pan for 5 minutes to cool, and transfer to a wire rack to cool completely. You will have some batter left over, so wash and dry the doughnut pan. Spray two cups and make two more doughnuts.

In a bowl set over a pan of barely simmering water, melt the chocolate. Dip the top of each doughnut in the chocolate and replace on the wire rack to drain. Sprinkle with sugar sprinkles to decorate and let set.

Makes 8

CHOCOLATE SAMOAS DRIZZLED WITH CARAMEL AND DARK CHOCOLATE

These quickly made little doughnuts are flavored with cinnamon, deep-fried, and topped with caramel glaze, toasted coconut, and chocolate.

INGREDIENTS

For the doughnuts
- 1 ½ cups (190g) all-purpose flour
- 2 tablespoons cornstarch
- 1 teaspoon baking powder
- ½ teaspoon salt
- 1 teaspoon ground cinnamon
- ⅓ cup (70g) brown sugar
- ¼ cup (50g) superfine sugar
- 2 tablespoons (30g) unsalted butter
- 1 large egg, room temperature, lightly beaten
- ⅓ cup (80ml) whole milk
- Vegetable oil for deep-frying

For the glaze
- 2 ½ tablespoons whole milk
- 3 tablespoons (45g) salted butter
- 1 ½ tablespoons superfine sugar
- 1 cup (100g) powdered sugar, sifted

For the decoration
- ½ cup (75g) sweetened coconut flakes
- 4 ounces (115g) semisweet chocolate, melted

METHOD

Combine the flour, cornstarch, baking powder, salt, and cinnamon in a large bowl. In a separate bowl, whisk the brown sugar, white sugar, and butter together until light and fluffy. Add the egg a little at a time, and continue whisking until incorporated. Alternately add the flour mixture and the milk until well mixed. The mixture will be quite sticky. Cover and refrigerate for 2–24 hours.

Transfer the dough to a lightly floured work surface and roll out to ⅜-inch (1cm) thickness. Using a 1 ½-inch (3.75cm) doughnut cutter, cut out 18 doughnuts, rerolling the dough as necessary.

Heat the oil in a heavy, large pan to 360°F (182°C). Fry the doughnuts in batches for just over 1 minute on each side, remove, and drain on paper towels. Cool on a wire rack.

Make the glaze. In a small pan, warm the milk and butter. In a separate pan over a medium heat, cook the sugar for a few minutes, stirring occasionally, until it becomes caramel. Add milk mixture and stir over a gentle heat until caramel has dissolved. Gradually add the powdered sugar until it is the perfect consistency for dipping. Keep over a low heat and stir occasionally to keep it runny.

In a large skillet, toast the flaked coconut over medium heat until mostly light golden brown.

Dip top of each doughnut in the glaze, set on the wire rack, and sprinkle with the coconut flakes. Using a disposable pastry bag or a plastic bag with the corner cut off, drizzle the melted chocolate back and forth over the doughnuts to decorate. Serve immediately.

Makes 18

CHOCOLATE AND COCONUT SNOWBALLS

Chocolate and coconut are a classic combination—not too sweet and with a wonderfully crisp texture to bite into. Choose 60 percent or higher cocoa powder to get the rich chocolate undertones in this doughnut.

INGREDIENTS

For the doughnuts
- 2 ½ cups (250g) all-purpose flour
- ¼ cup (50g) superfine sugar
- 2 packages (4 ½ teaspoons) active dry yeast
- 1 teaspoon salt
- 9 tablespoons whole milk, warmed
- 6 tablespoons warm water
- 2 large eggs, room temperature, lightly beaten
- ¼ cup (60g) unsalted butter, room temperature
- Vegetable oil for deep-frying
- ½ cup (170g) strawberry or raspberry preserves

For the frosting
- 2 cups (200g) powdered sugar, sifted
- ¼ cup (20g) unsweetened cocoa powder, sifted
- 1 tablespoon salted butter, softened
- ½ cup (120ml) whole milk
- 1 ½ cups (220g) sweetened coconut flakes

METHOD

Line two large cookie sheets with parchment paper.

In the bowl of a stand mixer, combine the flour and sugar. Add the yeast on one side and the salt on the other. Make a well in the center, and add the milk, water, and eggs. Using the dough hook attachment, mix until the dough comes together. Add the butter and continue to mix, until you have a slightly sticky dough. If too dry, add more water; if too wet, add more flour. Mix on medium speed for about 5–8 minutes, until the dough is smooth and elastic. Transfer to a large lightly oiled bowl, cover, and leave for an hour.

Transfer dough to a lightly floured work surface and punch down. Divide the dough into 20 pieces, and shape each piece into a ball by folding the edges of the dough underneath and pinching the dough together. Place the doughnuts an inch (2.5cm) apart on the cookie sheets, cover with oiled plastic wrap, and leave for 45 minutes.

In a heavy, large pan, heat the oil to 360°F (182°C). Fry the doughnuts for about 2–3 minutes on each side. Drain on paper towels. In a small pan over a gentle heat, warm the preserves, then push through a sieve to remove the seeds. Fill a disposable pastry bag fitted with a long tip with the preserves, and pipe into the center of each doughnut, being careful not to overfill.

Make the frosting. Place the powdered sugar and cocoa powder in a heatproof bowl and stir in the butter and milk. Set bowl over a pan of barely simmering water, and stir until smooth and thick enough for dipping. Remove from heat. Holding each doughnut between two forks, dip into the icing, and roll in the coconut flakes. Place on a wire rack until set.

Makes 20

BAKED GLUTEN-FREE CHOCOLATE DOUGHNUTS WITH BUTTERSCOTCH GLAZE

You would not guess that these tasty doughnuts are wheat- and gluten-free.

INGREDIENTS

For the doughnuts
- ½ cup (60g) white rice flour
- ⅓ cup (40g) tapioca flour
- ⅓ cup (40g) potato starch
- 2 tablespoons unsweetened cocoa powder, sifted
- ½ cup (100g) superfine sugar
- 1 teaspoon baking powder
- 1 teaspoon xanthan gum or CMC powder
- 1 teaspoon ground cinnamon
- ¼ teaspoon salt
- 2 tablespoons semisweet chocolate chips
- ¼ cup (60g) salted butter, melted
- 1 large egg, room temperature
- 2 tablespoons buttermilk
- 1 large ripe banana, mashed

For the glaze
- ¼ cup (60ml) whole milk
- 1 ⅓ cups (130g) powdered sugar, sifted
- ¼ cup (80g) butterscotch chips

For the decoration
- ¼ cup (80g) semisweet chocolate chips, melted

METHOD

Preheat the oven to 350°F (175°C) and spray a 6-cup doughnut pan with oil.

In a large bowl, whisk together the flours and potato starch, cocoa powder, sugar, baking powder, xanthan gum, cinnamon, and salt. Stir in the chocolate chips. Make a well in the center and add the melted butter, beaten egg, buttermilk, and banana. Mix well.

Pipe or spoon the batter into the doughnut pan, filling the cups two-thirds full. Bake for 12 minutes, let cool in the pan for 5 minutes, and transfer to a wire rack to cool completely. Wash and dry the doughnut pan, then spray two cups to make two more doughnuts with the remaining batter.

Make the glaze. Heat the milk in a small pan, and over medium heat until just below a simmer, and add the powdered sugar a tablespoon at a time until it is all incorporated. Add the butterscotch chips and keep heating and stirring until melted and the glaze is smooth. Keep warm over a low heat, stirring occasionally to keep it runny. Add a little more milk if the glaze becomes too thick.

Dip the top of each doughnut in the glaze and return to the rack to drain. Drizzle each one decoratively with the melted semisweet chocolate, using a pastry bag or a plastic bag with the corner cut off. Let set.

Makes 8

RICH CHOCOLATE DOUGHNUTS WITH BUTTERSCOTCH AND SALTED PEANUTS

Sweet meets salty in this heavenly matchup. Why not dunk it in some hot coffee?

INGREDIENTS

For the doughnuts
- 2 tablespoons active dry yeast
- 1 cup (240ml) whole milk, warmed
- ½ cup (60g) white bread flour
- 3 cups (375g) all-purpose flour
- ¼ cup (60g) cold unsalted butter, grated
- 1 teaspoon vanilla extract
- 2 large eggs
- 1 large egg yolk
- 2 tablespoons plain yogurt
- ¼ cup (50g) superfine sugar
- ½ teaspoon salt
- Vegetable oil for deep-frying

For the chocolate glaze
- ¼ cup (60ml) heavy cream
- 3 tablespoons (45g) cold unsalted butter, grated
- ⅙ cup (40ml) light corn syrup
- 3 ounces (85g) bittersweet chocolate, coarsely chopped
- ½ teaspoon vanilla extract
- ½ cup (60g) chopped salted peanuts

For the butterscotch glaze
- ¼ cup (25g) powdered sugar, sifted
- 1 ¼ tablespoons (20g) cold unsalted butter, grated
- ¼ cup (60ml) heavy cream
- ¼ cup (80g) butterscotch chips

METHOD

In a large mixing bowl, dissolve yeast in milk. Add the bread flour and 1 ½ cups (190g) all-purpose flour. Mix in a stand mixer with the paddle attachment until smooth. Cover and let rest for 20 minutes. Gradually add the butter and mix until incorporated. Add the vanilla, eggs, egg yolk, and yogurt. Turn off mixer, add the sugar and salt, then mix on low until the dough starts to come together.

With the dough hook attachment, add the remaining flour in three stages. The dough should pull away from the sides of the bowl nicely, but still be sticky. Cover and set in a warm place for 30 minutes. Gently press the dough down with your fist and let sit again for 1 hour, or until doubled.

On a lightly floured surface, roll dough ½ inch (1.25cm) thick. Cut rounds using a 3 ½-inch (8.75cm) doughnut cutter, place on floured cookie sheets, cover with oiled plastic wrap, and let rise for 15 minutes.

Heat the oil in a large, heavy pan to 360°F (182°C). Fry a few doughnuts at a time for 2 minutes per side, remove, and drain on paper towels.

Make chocolate glaze. Over low heat, stir heavy cream, butter, and corn syrup. After 2 minutes, add chocolate and continue to stir. When mixture reaches desired consistency, take pan off heat, add vanilla, and stir for 1 minute. Dip doughnut tops in warm glaze and place on paper towels to set. While glaze is still warm, sprinkle with peanuts.

Make butterscotch glaze. Mix powdered sugar, grated butter, and heavy cream. Heat butterscotch chips in microwave in 30-second intervals until the chips are half melted. Remove and stir until fully melted. Stir in sugar mixture. Drizzle butterscotch decoratively on the doughnuts. Let set before serving.

Makes about 12

PEANUT BUTTER DOUGHNUTS WITH CHOCOLATE GANACHE

This doughnut is the peanut butter cup's cousin, made better with a fluffy inside.
You'll never want to eat anything else.

INGREDIENTS

For the doughnuts
- 2 tablespoons active dry yeast
- 1 cup (240ml) whole milk, warmed
- ½ cup (60g) white bread flour
- 3 cups (375g) all-purpose flour
- ¼ cup (60g) cold unsalted butter, grated
- 1 teaspoon vanilla extract
- 2 large eggs
- 1 large egg yolk
- 2 tablespoons plain yogurt
- ¼ cup (50g) superfine sugar
- ½ teaspoon salt
- Vegetable oil for deep-frying

For the filling
- 1 cup (260g) smooth peanut butter
- 2 ½ cups (250g) powdered sugar, sifted
- 1 teaspoon vanilla extract
- 4 tablespoons heavy cream

For the ganache
- 2 ounces (60g) dark chocolate, coarsely chopped
- ¼ cup (60ml) heavy cream
- ¼ tablespoon (5g) unsalted butter

For the decoration
- Chopped peanuts

METHOD

In a large mixing bowl, dissolve yeast in milk. Add the bread flour and 1 ½ cups (190g) all-purpose flour. Mix in a stand mixer with the paddle attachment until smooth. Cover and let rest for 20 minutes. Gradually add the butter and mix until incorporated. Add the vanilla, eggs, egg yolk, and yogurt. Turn off mixer, add the sugar and salt, then mix on low until the dough starts to come together.

With the dough hook attachment, add the remaining flour in three stages. The dough should pull away from the sides of the bowl, but still be slightly sticky. If too wet, add a little more flour. Cover and set in a warm place for 30 minutes. Gently press the dough down with your fist and let sit again for 1 hour, or until the dough has doubled.

On a lightly floured surface, roll dough ½ inch (1.25cm) thick. Cut rounds using a 3 ½-inch (8.75cm) biscuit cutter, place on floured cookie sheets, cover with oiled plastic wrap, and let rise for 15 minutes.

Make the filling while the doughnuts are rising. In the bowl of a stand mixer, beat the filling ingredients on medium speed for 2–3 minutes. Chill.

Heat the oil in a large, heavy pan to 360°F (182°C). Fry doughnuts for 3 minutes on first side, 2 minutes on the other side, remove, and drain on paper towels.

Make ganache. Place chocolate in a bowl. Heat cream to a low boil, then pour over the chocolate until it begins to melt. Add butter and stir until smooth. Dip the doughnut tops in the ganache and set on paper towels. While the ganache is still warm, sprinkle with peanuts, if desired.

Before serving, slice doughnuts in half and fill with peanut butter filling.

Makes about 12

TRIPLE CHOCOLATE DOUGHNUTS WITH BROWNIE TOPPING

Is there such thing as too much chocolate? Definitely not! This doughnut is proof!

INGREDIENTS

For the doughnuts
- ¼ cup (50g) superfine sugar
- 1 large egg
- 1 tablespoon active dry yeast
- 1 cup (240ml) whole milk, warmed
- ½ tablespoon vanilla extract
- ⅔ cup (60g) unsweetened cocoa powder
- 1 teaspoon salt
- 1 teaspoon baking soda
- ¾ cup (240g) white chocolate chips
- 3 cups (375g) all-purpose flour
- ½ cup (115g) cold unsalted butter, grated

For the ganache
- 2 ounces (60g) dark chocolate, coarsely chopped
- ¼ cup (60ml) heavy cream
- ¼ tablespoon (5g) unsalted butter

For the decoration
- 1 cup (100g) coarsely chopped brownies
- Chocolate sprinkles or shavings (optional)

METHOD

In the bowl of a stand mixer with the paddle attachment, beat sugar and eggs until blended. Add the yeast, milk, vanilla, cocoa powder, salt, baking soda, and chocolate chips. Stir to blend. With the mixer on low, add 2 cups (250g) flour, ½ cup (60g) at a time, until the dough pulls away from the sides of the bowl.

Switching to the dough hook, slowly add the butter until fully incorporated. On low speed, add the remaining flour. The dough should now be soft, but not too sticky. Knead the dough gently on a lightly floured surface until it is no longer sticky. Butter the inside of a bowl and place the dough ball inside. Cover with plastic wrap and allow the dough to double in size, about 45 minutes.

Preheat oven to 375°F (190°C) and place parchment on large cookie sheets. Gently press dough down with your fist and roll out ½ inch (1.25cm) thick. Cut out doughnuts with a 3 ½-inch (8.75cm) doughnut cutter and set an inch (2.5cm) apart on cookie sheets. Cover with oiled plastic wrap and let rise until doubled, about 15 minutes. Bake for 10–12 minutes or until doughnuts spring back at the touch. Let cool on pans for 1 minute, then transfer to cooling racks.

Make ganache. Place chocolate in a bowl. Heat cream to a low boil, then pour over the chocolate until it begins to melt. Add butter and stir until smooth. Dip doughnut tops in the ganache and set on paper towels. While the ganache is still warm, sprinkle with the chopped brownies, and if desired, chocolate sprinkles or chocolate shavings.

Makes about 12

SPICY HOT CHOCOLATE DOUGHNUTS WITH MARSHMALLOW GLAZE

This is not your typical hot chocolate. Packing some heat, this doughnut is perfect for eating while in front of the fireplace.

INGREDIENTS

For the doughnuts
- 1 ½ cups (190g) all-purpose flour
- ¼ cup (20g) unsweetened cocoa powder
- 1 cup (200g) superfine sugar
- 1 teaspoon baking soda
- ½ teaspoon salt
- ⅛ teaspoon ground cayenne pepper, or to taste
- ¼ cup (60ml) plus 2 tablespoons vegetable oil
- 1 tablespoon white vinegar
- 1 cup (240ml) cold water
- 1 ½ teaspoons vanilla extract

For the glaze
- ¾ cup (75g) powdered sugar, sifted
- 2 tablespoons heavy cream
- 2 tablespoons (30g) unsalted butter, cubed or grated
- 1 ¼ cups (100g) mini marshmallows

For the decoration (optional)
- Chocolate shavings

METHOD

Preheat oven to 350°F (175°C). Using a nonstick spray, spray two 6-cup doughnut pans.

In the bowl of a stand mixer, combine the flour, cocoa, sugar, baking soda, salt, and cayenne pepper. On low speed, slowly add the oil, water, vanilla, and vinegar. Mix until smooth. The batter will be thin.

Spoon the batter into the doughnut pan, filling the cups three-quarters full. Bake for 10–12 minutes, or until a toothpick inserted in the center comes out clean. Let cool in the pans for 5 minutes, then carefully transfer doughnuts to a cooling rack to cool.

Make the marshmallow glaze. In a medium pan, whisk together the powdered sugar and heavy cream. Place pan over medium-low heat, whisking continually. After 1 minute, add the butter. Once the butter has melted, add the marshmallows slowly and continue to stir with a wooden spoon to the desired consistency. Working quickly, dip the tops of the cooled doughnuts in the marshmallow glaze and place on paper towels. If desired, sprinkle tops with chocolate shavings while the glaze is still warm.

Makes 12

MOCHA DOUGHNUTS WITH MOCHA GLAZE AND SHAVED CHOCOLATE

Coffee and chocolate. Need we say more?

INGREDIENTS

For the doughnuts
- 2 tablespoons active dry yeast
- ¾ cup (180ml) whole milk, warmed
- ¼ cup (60ml) espresso, warmed
- ½ cup (60g) white bread flour
- 2 ½ cups (250g) all-purpose flour
- ½ cup (45g) unsweetened cocoa powder
- ¼ cup (60g) cold unsalted butter, grated
- 2 large eggs
- 1 large egg yolk
- 2 tablespoons plain yogurt
- 1 teaspoon vanilla extract
- ¼ cup (50g) superfine sugar
- ¾ teaspoon baking powder
- 1 ½ teaspoons salt
- Vegetable oil for deep-frying

For the glaze
- ½ cup (50g) powdered sugar, sifted
- ¼ cup (20g) unsweetened cocoa powder
- 1 tablespoon heavy cream
- 1 tablespoon espresso

For the decoration
- ¼ cup (80g) chocolate shavings

METHOD

In a large mixing bowl, dissolve yeast in milk and espresso. Add the bread flour, 1 cup (125g) all-purpose flour, and cocoa powder. Mix in a stand mixer with the paddle attachment until smooth. Cover and let rest for 20 minutes.

Gradually add the butter to the dough and mix until incorporated. Then add the eggs, egg yolk, yogurt, and vanilla extract. Turn off mixer and add the sugar, baking powder, and salt. Mix on low until the dough starts to come together.

With the dough hook attachment, add the remaining flour in three stages. The dough should pull away from the sides of the bowl nicely, but still be slightly sticky. If too wet, add a little more flour. Cover and set in a warm place for 30 minutes. Gently press dough down with your fist and let sit again for 1 hour, or until dough has doubled.

Turn dough out onto a lightly floured surface and roll ½ inch (1.25cm) thick. Cut rounds using a 3 ½-inch (8.75cm) doughnut cutter, place an inch (2.5cm) apart on floured cookie sheets, cover with oiled plastic wrap, and let rise for 15 minutes.

Heat the oil in a large, heavy pan to 360°F (182°C). Fry a few doughnuts at a time for 2 minutes per side, remove with a slotted spoon, and place on paper towels.

Make the mocha glaze. Whisk together the powdered sugar, cocoa powder, heavy cream, and espresso. Add more powdered sugar or espresso, depending on your preference. When the glaze is smooth, dip the doughnut tops in it. Set doughnuts on paper towels. Before the glaze has fully set, sprinkle with chocolate shavings.

Makes about 12

CHOCOLATE DOUGHNUTS WITH CHOCOLATE-RASPBERRY GLAZE

Nothing is better than chocolate-covered berries.
Except maybe chocolate-and-berry-covered doughnuts!

INGREDIENTS

For the doughnuts
- 1 large egg
- ¼ cup (50g) superfine sugar
- 1 tablespoon active dry yeast
- 1 cup (240ml) whole milk, warmed
- ½ tablespoon vanilla extract
- ⅔ cup (60g) unsweetened cocoa powder
- 1 teaspoon salt
- 1 teaspoon baking soda
- 3 cups (375g) all-purpose flour
- ½ cup (115g) cold unsalted butter, grated

For the glaze
- ½ cup (50g) powdered sugar, sifted
- ¼ cup (20g) unsweetened cocoa powder
- 2 tablespoons heavy cream
- 2 tablespoons raspberry preserves, or to taste

For the decoration (optional)
- Handful of fresh raspberries

METHOD

In the bowl of a stand mixer with the paddle attachment, beat eggs and sugar until blended. Add the yeast, milk, vanilla, cocoa powder, salt, and baking soda, and stir until blended. With the mixer on low, add 2 cups (250g) flour, ½ cup (60g) at a time, until the dough pulls away from the sides of the bowl.

Switching to the dough hook, slowly add the butter until fully incorporated. On low speed, add the remaining flour. The dough should now be soft, but not too sticky. Continue to mix the dough with the dough hook until it is no longer sticky. Butter the inside of a bowl and place the dough ball inside. Cover with plastic wrap and allow the dough to double in size, about 45 minutes.

Preheat oven to 375°F (190°C) and place parchment paper on large cookie sheets. Gently press dough down with your fist and roll out ½ inch (1.25cm) thick. Cut out doughnuts with a 3 ½-inch (8.75cm) doughnut cutter and set an inch (2.5cm) apart on cookie sheets. Cover with oiled plastic wrap and let rise until doubled, about 15 minutes. Bake for 10–12 minutes or until doughnuts spring back at the touch. Let cool on pans for 1 minute, then transfer to cooling racks.

Make the glaze. In a medium bowl, whisk together the powdered sugar, cocoa powder, and heavy cream. When smooth, mix in the raspberry preserves. You may add more or less of the preserves, according to your preference. Dip the tops of the doughnuts in the glaze and let set on paper towels.

If you like, coarsely chop some fresh raspberries and sprinkle them on top of the newly glazed doughnuts.

Makes about 12

Chapter 6

ALL AROUND THE WORLD

Why bother spending a lot of money on traveling, when all you really want is to sample the cuisine? We've gathered some unique and scrumptious fried delights from all over the globe. Whether you might fancy the sweetly simple Canadian fried dough or the purely indulgent take on Turkish delight, we've got you covered.

MEXICAN CHURROS WITH HOT CHOCOLATE DIP

Churros are sausage-shaped doughnuts that are meant for plunging in the thick chocolate sauce served with them. They're traditional favorites for breakfast in Mexico and Spain, but you can enjoy them at any time of the day.

INGREDIENTS

For the churros
- ⅔ cup (160ml) water
- 4 tablespoons vegetable oil
- ½ cup (60g) all-purpose flour
- Pinch salt
- 2 large eggs, room temperature
- Vegetable oil for deep-frying
- ¼ cup (50g) superfine sugar

For the dipping sauce
- 2 ounces (60g) semisweet chocolate
- ⅔ cup (160ml) heavy cream

METHOD

Place the water in a saucepan with 4 tablespoons oil and bring to a boil. Mix the flour with the salt and gradually add it to the boiling water. Stir well with a wooden spoon over low heat until the mixture sticks together and leaves the sides of the pan. Remove from the heat and beat in the eggs.

In a heavy, large pan, heat the oil to 360°F (182°C). Spoon the churros mixture into a pastry bag fitted with a large star-shaped tip. Pipe two or three 4-inch (10cm) lengths of dough at a time directly into the hot oil and cook for 2 minutes on each side, until crisp and golden. Drain the churros on paper towels and sprinkle with sugar. Repeat until all the churros mixture is used up.

To make the chocolate dip, gently warm the chocolate and cream together in a small saucepan. Stir until smooth, remove it from the heat, and transfer to a small bowl. Serve with a pile of the hot churros. Serve immediately.

Makes 12

POLISH PACZKI WITH RASPBERRY FILLING

These are filled with raspberry preserves and dusted all over with powdered sugar.

INGREDIENTS

For the starter
- 2 cups (475ml) whole milk, warmed
- 1 teaspoon superfine sugar
- 2 packages (4 ½ teaspoons) instant yeast
- 1 cup (125g) all-purpose flour
- 1 cup (125g) white bread flour

For the doughnuts
- 1 large egg, room temperature
- 4 large egg yolks, room temperature
- ½ cup (100g) superfine sugar
- 1 teaspoon salt
- 1 teaspoon vanilla extract
- ¼ cup (60g) salted butter, melted and cooled slightly
- 3 cups (375g) all-purpose flour
- ⅔ cup (225g) raspberry preserves
- Vegetable oil for deep-frying

For the decoration
- 1 cup (100g) powdered sugar, sifted

METHOD

Line two large cookie sheets with parchment paper.

Make the starter. Put the warm milk in the bowl of a stand mixer, stir in 1 teaspoon superfine sugar, and sprinkle the yeast on top. Leave for 5 minutes, then add 1 cup (125g) all-purpose flour and 1 cup (125g) white bread flour. Mix with the paddle attachment until the mixture becomes a thick batter. Cover the bowl with plastic wrap and leave somewhere warm for 30 minutes, until plenty of bubbles appear on the surface.

In a large bowl, whisk the egg, egg yolks, sugar, salt, and vanilla until light. Change to the dough hook, add the melted and cooled butter to the starter, and mix until combined. Slowly add the egg mixture, mixing well. Add the 3 cups flour (375g), ½ cup (60g) at a time, until a soft and sticky dough is formed. Cover bowl with plastic wrap and place somewhere warm for an hour, until doubled in size.

Transfer the dough to a lightly floured work surface. Punch dough down, divide into 18 equal pieces, and flatten out each one slightly. Spoon a generous teaspoon of raspberry preserves into the middle of each piece and fold up the dough around the filling, pinching well to seal it. Place 1 inch (2.5cm) apart on the cookie sheets, seam underneath. Cover with plastic wrap that has been sprayed with oil and leave somewhere warm for an hour until slightly risen.

Heat the oil in a heavy, large pan to 360°F (182°C). Fry the doughnuts for 3 minutes on first side, 2 minutes on second side, and drain on the paper towels. Place the sugar in a wide shallow bowl. Roll each doughnut in the sugar and serve warm.

Makes 18

DUTCH OLLIEBOLLEN

The dried fruit and apple in these little doughnuts make every bite a taste sensation.

INGREDIENTS

For the doughnuts
- 1 cup (240ml) whole milk, warmed
- 1 tablespoon superfine sugar
- 1 package (2 ¼ teaspoons) active dry yeast
- 2 ¼ cups (280g) all-purpose flour
- 1 teaspoon salt
- 1 large egg, room temperature, lightly beaten
- 1 tart green apple, peeled, cored, and finely chopped
- ¾ cup (90g) raisins
- ¾ cup (90g) dried currants
- Vegetable oil for deep-frying

For the decoration
- ½ cup (50g) powdered sugar, sifted

METHOD

Place the warm milk in a medium bowl, stir in the sugar, sprinkle the yeast on top, and leave for 10–15 minutes, until frothy.

Place the flour and salt in the bowl of a stand mixer, make a well in the center, and pour in the yeast liquid and beaten egg. Using the dough hook attachment, mix on medium speed until a dough comes together. Add the chopped apple, raisins, and currants, and mix well until combined. Cover the bowl and leave in a warm place for an hour, until dough has doubled in size.

Heat the oil in a heavy, large pan to 360°F (182°C). Remove the cover from the bowl, and place the bowl next to the pan with the hot oil.

Now you are going to use two metal spoons to shape the dough into balls. Dip the spoons quickly in and out of the hot oil, and using one spoon, scoop out a piece of dough slightly smaller than a golf ball. Using the other spoon, mold the dough quickly into a ball shape, and lower it into the oil. Fry each ball for about 2 minutes on each side, or until golden brown. Do not overcrowd the pan, as this lowers the temperature of the oil too much.

Drain the doughnuts on paper towels, and serve warm, dusted with powdered sugar.

Makes 12

TURKISH DELIGHT WITH HONEY AND ROSEHIP SYRUP AND CARAMELIZED PECANS

Middle Eastern bakers bring a unique flair to the world of doughnuts. Filled with Turkish Delight candy, these are served with an aromatic syrup and topped with crunchy caramelized pecans.

INGREDIENTS

For the syrup
- 7 ounces (200g) honey
- 1 cinnamon stick
- ¼ cup (60ml) rosewater
- 1 teaspoon vanilla extract

For the doughnuts
- 3 ¾ cups (470g) all-purpose flour
- 1 tablespoon superfine sugar
- 2 packages (4 ½ teaspoons) instant yeast
- ½ teaspoon salt
- 1 ½ cups (360ml) warm water
- 4 ounces (115g) Turkish Delight candy, cut into ½-inch (1.25cm) pieces
- Vegetable oil for deep-frying

For the topping
- ¼ cup (60g) salted butter
- ¼ cup (50g) superfine sugar
- ⅔ cup (80g) chopped pecans

METHOD

Make the syrup. Heat the honey and cinnamon stick gently in a small pan until runny. Remove from the heat, add the rosewater and vanilla, and set aside to cool.

With the dough hook, in the bowl of a stand mixer, combine the flour and sugar. Add the yeast on one side and the salt on the other. Make a well in the center and pour in the warm water. Mix until the dough comes together, adding more water if too dry or more flour if too wet. Knead for 5–8 minutes, until the dough is smooth and elastic. Transfer to a large lightly oiled bowl, cover, and leave for an hour.

Make the caramelized pecans. In a small pan, melt the butter and add the sugar. Increase the heat and cook until the sugar has caramelized. Stir in the pecans, remove from the heat, and set aside to cool.

Transfer dough to a lightly floured work surface and punch down. Divide into 12 pieces and flatten out each one. Place a piece of Turkish Delight in the middle of each one and fold up the edges of the dough around it, to form a ball. Pinch well to seal.

In a heavy, large pan, heat the oil to 360°F (182°C), and fry the doughnuts for 3 minutes on first side, and 2 minutes second side. Drain on paper towels.

Make the caramelized pecan topping. In a small pan, melt the butter and add the sugar. Increase the heat and cook until the sugar has caramelized. Stir in the pecans, remove from the heat, and set aside to cool.

To serve, place the warm doughnuts on a serving dish and pour the syrup over and around them, leaving the cinnamon stick poking out between the balls. Scatter the caramelized nuts over the top.

Makes 12

CHOCOLATE BEIGNETS WITH CHOCOLATE SAUCE

Little pastry pockets filled with chocolate cream, and served with warm chocolate sauce, these are delectable at any time of the day.

INGREDIENTS

For the doughnuts
- ¾ cup (180ml) warm water
- ¼ cup (50g) superfine sugar
- 1 package (2 ¼ teaspoons) active dry yeast
- 1 large egg, room temperature
- ½ teaspoon salt
- ½ cup (120ml) evaporated milk
- 3 ½ cups (440g) white bread flour
- 2 tablespoons (30g) salted butter, room temperature, diced
- Vegetable oil for deep-frying

For the dipping sauce
- 1 ¼ tablespoons (20g) salted butter
- ¼ cup (60g) chocolate spread
- ⅓ cup (80ml) whole milk

For the filling
- ⅓ cup (75g) chocolate spread

For the decoration
- ½ cup (50g) powdered sugar, sifted, for dusting

METHOD

Place the warm water in the bowl of a stand mixer, stir in the sugar, sprinkle the yeast on top, and leave for 10–15 minutes.

In a separate bowl, beat the egg, salt, and evaporated milk. Pour into the yeast liquid and stir to combine. Add 1 ½ cups (190g) flour and mix on low speed with the dough hook until combined. Add the butter a piece at a time, mixing well after each addition. Add the rest of the flour a little at a time, until you have a soft and sticky dough. If it still feels too sticky, add a little more flour. Cover with plastic wrap and leave for an hour.

Make the chocolate sauce. In a small pan over a gentle heat, melt the butter, add the chocolate spread and the milk, and whisk until smooth. Set aside.

Transfer the dough to a lightly floured work surface, punch down, and roll out to a ⅛-inch (3mm) thick square. Cut into 3 x 3-inch (7.5 x 7.5cm) squares, about 24. Place a generous teaspoon of chocolate spread in the middle of half of the squares. Top each one with a plain square. Pinch the edges together, fold each edge in about ¼ inch (6mm), and pinch again to ensure that each square is securely sealed.

Heat the oil in a heavy, large pan to 360°F (182°C). Fry the beignets in batches, for 2 minutes on each side, flipping them over occasionally. Drain on paper towels. Sprinkle with powdered sugar and serve warm with warm chocolate sauce.

Makes 12

GREEK-STYLE HONEY LOUKOUMADES

These innocent looking little doughnuts are amazing little puffs of air, delightfully smothered in honey syrup and sprinkled with walnuts.

INGREDIENTS

For the doughnuts
- 1 teaspoon superfine sugar
- 2 cups (475ml) warm water, divided
- 1 package (2 ¼ teaspoons) active dry yeast
- 3 cups (375g) all-purpose flour
- 1 teaspoon baking powder
- ½ teaspoon baking soda
- ½ teaspoon salt
- Vegetable oil for deep-frying

For the syrup
- 2 cups (400g) superfine sugar
- ½ teaspoon ground cinnamon
- 1 cup (240ml) water
- ½ cup (120ml) honey

For the decoration
- ¼ cup (30g) chopped walnuts

METHOD

Add the sugar to ½ cup (120ml) warm water, sprinkle the yeast on top, and set aside for 10–15 minutes, until frothy.

In a large bowl, whisk the flour, baking powder, baking soda, and salt together. Make a well in the center and add the yeast liquid and remaining 1 ½ cups (360ml) warm water, mixing well until it becomes a thick batter, with no lumps. Cover the bowl with plastic wrap and leave somewhere warm for an hour, until doubled in size.

Make the syrup. In a small pan, over medium heat, warm the sugar, cinnamon, water, and honey until the sugar has dissolved. Bring to a boil, then simmer gently for 3–4 minutes. Keep warm.

Heat the oil in a heavy, large pan to 360°F (182°C). Remove the cover from the bowl, and place the bowl next to the pan with the hot oil. You will need two metal spoons to shape the dough into balls. Dip the spoons quickly in and out of the hot oil, and using one spoon, scoop out about a teaspoon of dough. Using the other spoon, mold the dough quickly into a ball shape and lower it into the oil. Fry each ball for 1–2 minutes on each side, or until golden brown. Do not overcrowd the pan. Drain on paper towels.

Carefully dip the doughnuts in the hot syrup, place on a serving plate, and sprinkle with chopped walnuts. Serve immediately.

Makes about 35

FRENCH CRULLERS

These gorgeous little rum-glazed doughnuts are made with choux pastry,
piped into rings, and deep fried.

INGREDIENTS

For the doughnuts
- 1 cup (240ml) water
- ⅓ cup (75g) unsalted butter, plus extra for greasing
- 1 tablespoon superfine sugar
- ¼ teaspoon salt
- 1 cup (125g) all-purpose flour, sifted
- 3 large eggs, room temperature
- 1–2 large egg whites, room temperature, lightly beaten
- Vegetable oil for deep-frying

For the glaze
- 2 cups (200g) powdered sugar, sifted
- 2 tablespoons dark rum
- 1 tablespoon water

METHOD

Cut out 14 4-inch (10cm) squares of parchment paper, and draw a 3-inch (7.5cm) circle on each one to make piping the right size crullers easier. Butter each square lightly.

In a large pan, heat the water, butter, sugar, and salt, stirring until the sugar has dissolved. Bring the mixture to a boil, remove the pan from the heat, and add the flour all at once, stirring hard with a wooden spoon until it is completely incorporated and forms a ball. Return the pan to medium-low heat and cook, stirring continuously, to evaporate some of the moisture and the dough films in the bottom of the pan, about 1 ½ minutes. Transfer the mixture into a medium bowl and, using a handheld electric mixer, add the eggs, one at a time, ensuring they are completely incorporated before adding the next one. Scrape down the sides of the bowl occasionally.

Add just enough of the beaten egg whites, a little at a time, until the mixture is thick, smooth, and glossy; just holds its shape; and has a dropping consistency.

In a large, heavy pan, heat the oil to 360°F (182°C). Using a pastry bag with a large star nozzle, pipe 3-inch (7.5cm) doughnut rings onto the parchment squares. Turn the crullers into the hot oil carefully, sliding them off the paper squares. If the paper goes in the oil with the cruller, wait a moment, and using tongs, peel the square away from the cruller. Cook in batches for about 1 minute per side, or until golden brown, and drain on paper towels.

Make the glaze. Put the powdered sugar into a large bowl, and whisk in the rum and enough water to make a dipping consistency. Dip the top of each cruller in the glaze and place on a wire rack to set before serving.

Makes 14

TIP
For a different glaze, use lemon juice, or honey and heavy cream.

SOUR CHERRY DOUGHNUTS WITH AMARETTO GLAZE

Who needs a cannoli for dessert when you can have this beauty?
It's the perfect ending to a large Italian meal.

INGREDIENTS

For the filling
- ¼ cup (50g) superfine sugar
- 1 tablespoon tapioca starch (tapioca flour)
- Pinch salt
- 2 tablespoons fresh lemon juice
- 1 ½ cups (270g) fresh tart cherries, pitted and chopped

For the doughnuts
- 2 tablespoons active dry yeast
- 1 cup (240ml) whole milk, warmed
- ½ cup (60g) white bread flour
- 3 cups (375g) all-purpose flour
- ¼ cup (60g) cold unsalted butter, grated
- 1 teaspoon vanilla extract
- 2 large eggs
- 1 large egg yolk
- 2 tablespoons plain yogurt
- ¼ cup (50g) superfine sugar
- ½ teaspoon salt
- Vegetable oil for deep-frying

For the glaze
- 1 cup (100g) powdered sugar, sifted
- 3 tablespoons heavy cream
- 1 teaspoon amaretto liqueur
- ⅛ teaspoon almond extract

For the decoration (optional)
- Slivered almonds

METHOD

Make the filling. In a saucepan, stir the sugar, tapioca, and salt. Add lemon juice and cherries. Stir well and cook over medium heat for 2–3 minutes. Remove from heat and let cool. Refrigerate to chill and thicken. Can be made the day before.

In a large bowl, dissolve yeast in milk. Add the bread flour and 1 ½ cups (190g) all-purpose flour. Mix in a stand mixer with the paddle attachment until smooth. Cover and let rest for 20 minutes. Gradually add the butter and mix until incorporated. Add the vanilla, eggs, egg yolk, and yogurt. Turn off mixer, add the sugar and salt, then mix on low until the dough starts to come together.

With the dough hook, add the remaining flour in three stages. The dough should pull away from the sides of the bowl nicely, but still be slightly sticky. If too wet, add a little flour. Cover and set in a warm place for 30 minutes. Gently press dough down and let sit again for 1 hour, or until doubled. On a lightly floured surface, roll dough ½ inch (1.25cm) thick. Cut rounds with a 3 ½-inch (8.75cm) biscuit cutter (no hole in the center), place an inch (2.5cm) apart on floured cookie sheets, cover with oiled plastic wrap, and let rise for 15 minutes.

Heat the oil in a large, heavy pan to 360°F (182°C). Fry doughnuts for 3 minutes on first side, then 2 minutes on the other side, remove, and drain on paper towels. Let cool.

Make the glaze. In a medium bowl, whisk together the ingredients to a smooth spreading consistency.

Before serving, cut the doughnuts in half. Spread the filling over the bottom halves and replace the tops. Spread the glaze over the tops and sprinkle, if desired, with slivered almonds.

Makes about 12

FILLED MALASADAS

Originating in Portugal, these little doughy confections are eaten during Mardi Gras.
They are filled with anything from vanilla cream to guava preserves.

INGREDIENTS

For the doughnuts
- ½ cup (100g) superfine sugar
- 2 tablespoons warm water
- 1 tablespoon active dry yeast
- 3 large eggs
- 1 cup (240ml) evaporated milk
- 2 tablespoons (30g) cold unsalted butter, grated
- ¼ teaspoon salt
- 4 cups (500g) white bread flour
- Vegetable oil for deep-frying

For the filling and decoration
- 1 cup (340g) guava preserves (or use your favorite preserves)
- Sugar for rolling

METHOD

Dissolve 1 teaspoon of the sugar in the warm water. Lightly sprinkle the yeast on top and wait until foamy (3–5 minutes).

In the bowl of a stand mixer, beat the eggs until very thick. Add the yeast mixture, evaporated milk, remaining sugar, butter, and salt. Continue to mix until all ingredients are fully incorporated. Switching to the dough hook, add the flour in small increments until the dough starts to pull away from the edges of the bowl. It should be slightly sticky, but not too wet.

Cover the bowl and allow the dough to rise until doubled (about 1 hour). Turn the dough out onto a lightly floured surface and roll out to ½-inch (1.25cm) thickness. Cut out rounds using a 3 ½-inch (8.75cm) biscuit cutter (no hole in center). Place on parchment paper that has been lightly floured. Cover with oiled plastic wrap and allow to rise for 15 minutes.

Heat the oil in a heavy, large pan to 360°F (182°C). Gently place a few rounds in the pan at a time. Fry for 3 minutes on the first side, 2 minutes on the second side, then remove with a slotted spoon and place on paper towels to drain. While still warm, roll malasadas in sugar.

Once cooled, slide a knife in the side of a malasada and wiggle, creating a small opening. Place the preserves in a pastry bag with a large, round piping tip (or use a plastic bag with the corner cut off). Holding the malasada with one hand, slowly squeeze the bag until you can feel the preserves fill up the inside of the doughnut and they are ready to serve.

Makes 12–15

PICARONES WITH ORANGE BRANDY DIPPING SAUCE

Tired of plain old mashed sweet potatoes? Why not use them to make these yummy fried rings, hailing from Peru. If you want, you can substitute strong coffee for the brandy.

INGREDIENTS

For the doughnuts
- 1 ½ cinnamon sticks
- 1 ½ teaspoons whole anise seed
- 1 teaspoon whole cloves
- 2 large sweet potatoes, peeled and cubed
- ¾ cup (180g) canned pumpkin purée (not pumpkin pie filling)
- 1 tablespoon superfine sugar
- 1 tablespoon active dry yeast
- 2 large eggs
- 3 cups (375g) all-purpose flour
- Vegetable oil for deep-frying

For the dipping sauce
- ⅙ cup (60g) dark molasses
- 2 tablespoons brandy
- 1 ½ cups (300g) brown sugar
- 1 cinnamon stick
- Grated zest and juice of ½ orange

METHOD

In a large pot over high heat, bring a large amount of water to a boil. Add cinnamon sticks, anise seed, and cloves. Simmer for 10 minutes and remove the spices. Add the cubed sweet potatoes and cook until soft, then remove with a slotted spoon and cool. Mash the cooled potatoes with the pumpkin purée.

Reserve ½ cup (120ml) of the spiced water for the picarone dough.

In the bowl of a stand mixer, dissolve the sugar in the warm spiced water. Sprinkle the yeast on top and allow it to become foamy (about 5 minutes). Add the eggs and mashed pumpkin and squash mixture, and mix. Switching to the dough hook, add the flour gradually until it begins to pull away from the sides of the mixing bowl. Cover the bowl and allow the dough to double in size (about 1 ½–2 hours).

Make the dipping sauce. Mix all the ingredients in a medium saucepan. Bring to a boil while continually whisking. Once it starts to boil, lower the heat and allow mixture to simmer until slightly thickened (10–15 minutes). Remove from heat and allow to slightly cool. Remove cinnamon stick before serving.

Heat the oil in a heavy, large pot to 360°F (182°C).

Wet fingers and grab a tablespoonful of dough. Roll out into a long, thin, snake-like log, then pinch the ends together to make a ring. Drop a few at a time into the hot oil. Fry for 30 seconds on each side, remove with a slotted spoon, and place on paper towels to drain. Serve hot with the dipping sauce.

Makes about 15 rings

CANADIAN FRIED DOUGH

Called "beaver tails" by Canadians, these large sugar disks will keep you warm after snowshoeing all day. They are traditionally served with apple pie filling, but you'll enjoy them all on their own too!

INGREDIENTS

For the doughnuts
- ⅓ cup (65g) superfine sugar
- ½ cup (60ml) water, warmed
- 4 teaspoons active dry yeast
- 1 cup (240ml) whole milk, warmed
- 2 large eggs
- ⅓ cup (80ml) vegetable oil
- 1 teaspoon vanilla extract
- 1 ¼ teaspoons salt
- 4 cups (500g) all-purpose flour
- Vegetable oil for deep-frying

For the decoration and dipping sauce
- Sugar and ground cinnamon for dusting
- Canned apple pie filling for dipping (optional)

METHOD

Dissolve 1 teaspoon of the sugar in the warm water. Lightly sprinkle the yeast on top and wait until foamy (3–5 minutes).

In the bowl of a stand mixer, place the milk, eggs, ⅓ cup (80ml) oil, vanilla, remaining sugar, salt, and the yeast mixture. Mix for 2 minutes until smooth. Add the flour slowly until the dough pulls away from the sides of the bowl and forms a firm, but elastic ball. Cover and allow dough to rise until doubled in size, 30–40 minutes.

Gently press the dough down with your fist. Divide dough into 18 sections. Roll each section into an oval about 5 inches (12.75cm) long and ¼ inch (6mm) thick.

Heat the oil in a large, heavy pan to 375°F (190°C). Pick up a piece of dough and gently stretch it into a longer "beaver tail" shape (as long as you can fit into your pan). Place in the oil and fry until medium-brown for 2 minutes on first side, 1 ½ minutes on second side. Using a slotted spoon, remove the finished fried dough and place on paper towels to drain. Allow to cool only slightly.

Mix the desired amount of cinnamon and sugar in a large bowl. As soon as you can handle the fried dough, toss the pieces around in the cinnamon sugar to evenly coat both sides. Serve immediately, alone, or with apple pie filling if you wish.

Makes about 18

ITALIAN ZEPPOLE

With an amazingly surprising texture, these tiny treats are perfectly decadent alongside a coffee glaze (or an entire lasagna!).

INGREDIENTS

For the doughnuts
- 2 cups (250g) all-purpose flour
- ½ cup (100g) superfine sugar
- 2 tablespoons baking powder
- 1 teaspoon salt
- 2 large eggs
- 1 ½ cups (350g) ricotta cheese
- ½ cup (115g) mascarpone cheese
- ¼ cup (60ml) whole milk
- Vegetable oil for deep-frying

For the decoration and dipping sauce
- Powdered sugar for dusting
- 2 cups (625g) milk chocolate chips (optional)

METHOD

Heat the oil in a heavy, large pan to 360°F (182°C).

In a medium saucepan, place the flour, sugar, baking powder, salt, eggs, ricotta, mascarpone, and milk. Set the pan over low heat and whisk continually. The dough will be wet and will start to pull away from the sides of the pan. This takes around 4 minutes.

With a tablespoon, scoop spoonfuls of the warm dough and drop a few at a time in the hot oil. Fry until golden brown (3 minutes) and then flip to cook 2 ½ minutes on the other side. Remove with a slotted spoon and place on paper towels to drain and cool slightly. Dust with powdered sugar and serve.

Make a dipping sauce, if desired. Place the chocolate chips in a microwave-safe bowl. Heat in the microwave for 30-second intervals until half of the chips are melted. Remove from microwave and stir. Place in a bowl and serve with the warm zeppole.

Makes 24–30

VEGAN SOPAPILLAS

Originating in Mexico, sopapillas are perfect little pillows of crunchiness. It is so much fun to watch them puff as they fry! If being vegan isn't your thing, you may replace the coconut milk with whole milk; however, the coconut milk adds a wonderful taste.

INGREDIENTS

For the doughnuts
- 3 cups (375g) all-purpose flour
- 2 teaspoons baking powder
- 1 teaspoon salt
- ¼ cup (50g) vegetable shortening
- 1 cup (240ml) coconut milk, warmed
- Vegetable oil for deep-frying

For the decoration and dipping sauce
- Sugar for dusting (optional)
- Honey for dipping (optional)

METHOD

In a medium bowl, mix together the flour, baking powder, and salt. Cut in the shortening with either your fingers or a pastry cutter until the mixture resembles coarse sand. Add the coconut milk and mix.

Turn the dough out onto a lightly floured surface and knead until it is firm but slightly sticky. Place in a bowl, cover, and let rest for 30 minutes.

On a lightly floured surface, roll out the dough very thin, about ⅛ inch (3mm). With a knife or pizza cutter, cut the dough into small triangles.

Heat the oil in a heavy, large pan to 360°F (182°C). Gently place a few triangles in the pan at a time. Fry for about 1 minute on each side, until they reach a nice golden brown. Sopapillas should puff, but it is perfectly all right if they do not. Remove with a slotted spoon and place on paper towels.

If you want, while the sopapillas are still warm, dust with sugar and serve with honey for dipping.

Makes about 24

Chapter 7

YOU THOUGHT THESE WERE DESSERTS

This chapter takes traditional desserts and kicks them up a notch. Creating new twists on crème brûlée, rocky road, lemon meringue, and many more comfort dishes, any of these are sure to please. The mini versions also make a more sophisticated and surprising appearance for any dinner party.

LEMON MERINGUE DOUGHNUTS

The combination of flavors of soft doughnut, crispy meringue,
and tangy lemon curd are truly memorable.

INGREDIENTS

For the lemon curd
- 3 large eggs, room temperature
- Grated rind and juice of 2 large lemons
- ½ cup (115g) salted butter,
  room temperature
- 1 cup (200g) superfine sugar

For the doughnuts
- 2 cups (250g) all-purpose flour
- ¾ cup (150g) superfine sugar
- 2 teaspoons baking powder
- ½ teaspoon salt
- ¼ teaspoon baking soda
- 2 large eggs, room temperature
- ¾ cup (180ml) buttermilk
- 2 tablespoons (30g) unsalted butter,
  melted and cooled slightly
- 1 teaspoon vanilla extract
- Zest of 1 lemon

For the meringue
- 2 large egg whites, room temperature
- Pinch cream of tartar
- ½ cup (100g) superfine sugar, plus extra
  for sprinkling

METHOD

First make the lemon curd. Beat the eggs lightly in a medium bowl, and mix in the lemon rind and juice, butter, and sugar. Place the bowl over a pan of simmering water and heat gently, stirring occasionally, until the sugar has dissolved and the curd thickens. Pour into a clean, dry 16-ounce (450ml) jar and cover immediately.

Preheat the oven to 350°F (175°C) and spray two 6-cup doughnut pans with oil. In a large bowl, whisk together the flour, sugar, baking powder, baking soda, and salt. In a separate bowl, whisk the eggs, then add the buttermilk, butter, vanilla extract, and lemon zest. Pour into the flour mixture and stir until combined. Spoon or pipe the batter into the doughnut pans, filling the cups three-quarters full, slightly more than usual.

In a large, squeaky-clean bowl, whisk the egg whites until foamy. Add the cream of tartar and whisk until soft peaks form. Add the sugar a tablespoon at a time, whisking well until the mixture is stiff and glossy and holds its shape well. Pipe a thick swirl around the top of each doughnut, and sprinkle with a little sugar.

Bake for 12–13 minutes, or until a toothpick inserted in the center comes out clean. Remove from the oven and let cool in the pan for 5 minutes. Then run a thin knife around the edge of the doughnuts to loosen them, and carefully transfer them to a wire rack to cool completely.

To serve, place a generous teaspoon of lemon curd in the middle of each doughnut. Store any remaining lemon curd in the refrigerator.

Makes 12

TIP

Some substitutions for the lemon curd would be chocolate ganache (page 55) or a chocolate and peanut butter swirl (page 74). Or you could try a teaspoon of fruit preserves, topped with a few sliced strawberries or raspberries, with a swirl of whipped cream on top.

STICKY TOFFEE PUDDING DOUGHNUTS

*These sticky toffee doughnuts have a wonderful mixture of dates and molasses,
blended together in a delicious doughnut.*

INGREDIENTS

For the filling
- 8 ounces (225g) dried dates, pitted and finely chopped
- ¼ cup (60ml) water
- 1 tablespoon molasses
- 1 cup (125g) finely chopped walnuts

For the doughnuts
- ⅓ cup (80ml) warm water
- 1 teaspoon superfine sugar
- 1 package (2 ¼ teaspoons) active dry yeast
- 3 cups (375g) all-purpose flour
- ¾ cup (90g) white bread flour
- ½ cup (100g) superfine sugar
- 2 teaspoons salt
- ⅓ cup (80ml) whole milk, warmed
- 2 large eggs, room temperature, lightly beaten
- ½ cup (115g) salted butter, room temperature, cut into small pieces
- Vegetable oil for deep-frying

For the glaze
- ⅓ cup (80ml) whole milk
- ⅓ cup (75g) plus 1 tablespoon salted butter
- ¼ cup (50g) brown sugar
- 1 teaspoon vanilla extract

For the decoration
- 2 tablespoons chopped walnuts
- 1 ounce (30g) semisweet chocolate

METHOD

Line two large cookie sheets with parchment paper.

Make the sticky toffee filling. Over a gentle heat, stirring, mix dates and water until a thick paste is formed. Stir in molasses and walnuts and let cool.

Place the warm water in a medium bowl, stir in the teaspoon of sugar and the yeast, and leave for 10–15 minutes.

With the dough hook in the bowl of a stand mixer, stir both flours, ½ cup (100g) superfine sugar, and salt together. Add the yeast liquid, warm milk, and eggs, and mix until the dough comes together. On medium speed, add the pieces of butter, ensuring each piece is fully incorporated before adding the next, about 5–7 minutes. The dough should be slightly sticky. If it is too wet, add more flour; too dry, add more water. Transfer to a lightly oiled bowl, cover, and leave for an hour.

Transfer dough to a lightly floured work surface, knead twice, divide into 15 equal pieces, and flatten out each one. Spoon a generous teaspoon of sticky toffee into the middle of each piece and fold up the dough around the filling, sealing well. Place an inch (2.5cm) apart on the cookie sheets, seam underneath, cover with oiled plastic wrap, and leave for 30 minutes. Make glaze. Gently warm the milk and butter until melted. Add the brown sugar and vanilla, and stir until smooth.

Heat the oil in a heavy, large pan to 360°F (182°C). Fry the doughnuts for 3 minutes on the first side, 2 minutes on the other side. Drain on paper towels and cool on a wire rack. Dip the top of each doughnut in the glaze and set back on the rack. Immediately sprinkle a line of chopped walnuts down the center of each doughnut, and pipe a thin line of chocolate on either side of the nuts. Serve immediately.

Makes 15

CRÈME BRÛLÉE DOUGHNUTS

This doughnut is filled with homemade crème brûlée, adding an air of authenticity to the flavors.
It is best to make the brûlée the day before and chill it overnight.

INGREDIENTS

For the crème brûlée
- 2 large egg yolks
- 1 tablespoon superfine sugar
- 1 ⅓ cups (315ml) heavy cream
- ½ teaspoon vanilla extract

For the doughnuts
- ⅓ cup (80ml) warm water
- 1 teaspoon superfine sugar
- 1 package (2 ¼ teaspoons) active dry yeast
- 3 cups (375g) all-purpose flour
- ¾ cup (90g) white bread flour
- ½ cup (100g) superfine sugar
- 2 teaspoons salt
- ⅓ cup (80ml) whole milk, warmed
- 2 large eggs, room temperature,
  lightly beaten
- ½ cup (115g) salted butter, room
  temperature, cut into small pieces
- Vegetable oil for deep-frying

For the decoration
- 1 cup (200g) superfine sugar

METHOD

Preheat the oven to 350°F (175°C).

Make the crème brûlée the day before. In a small bowl, whisk the egg yolks and sugar. Warm the cream in a bowl over a pan of simmering water. Stir in the egg mixture. Continue cooking gently, stirring constantly, until thickened enough to coat the back of a spoon. Add the vanilla. Strain into 3 or 4 ramekin dishes and place in a roasting pan containing 1 inch (2.5cm) of water. Bake for 30–40 minutes. Remove, cool, cover, and refrigerate overnight.

Line two large cookie sheets with parchment paper.

Place the warm water in a medium bowl, stir in the teaspoon of sugar and the yeast, and leave for 10–15 minutes.

With the dough hook in the bowl of a stand mixer, stir both flours, ½ cup (100g) superfine sugar, and salt together. Add the yeast liquid, warm milk, and eggs, and mix until the dough comes together. On medium speed, add the butter pieces, ensuring each is fully incorporated before you add the next, about 5–7 minutes. The dough should be slightly sticky. If it is too wet, add more flour; too dry, add more water. Transfer to a lightly oiled bowl, cover, and leave for an hour.

On a lightly floured work surface, knead dough twice, divide into 15 equal pieces, and flatten out each one. Spoon a generous teaspoon of crème brûlée into the middle of each piece and fold up the dough around the filling, sealing well. Place an inch (2.5cm) apart on the cookie sheets, seam underneath, cover with oiled plastic wrap, and leave for 30 minutes. Heat the oil in a heavy, large pan to 360°F (182°C). Fry the doughnuts for 3 minutes on the first side, 2 minutes on the second, until golden brown. Drain on paper towels until cool enough to handle and roll in the sugar. Cool on a wire rack. Using a chef's blowtorch, caramelize the top of each doughnut.

Makes 15

DEATH BY CHOCOLATE

This chocolate doughnut, topped with a rich whipped chocolate ganache,
will satisfy even the biggest chocoholic.

INGREDIENTS

For the doughnuts
- 1 ¾ cups (220g) all-purpose flour
- ¾ cup (150g) superfine sugar
- 3 tablespoons unsweetened cocoa
  powder, sifted
- 2 teaspoons baking powder
- 1 teaspoon ground cinnamon
- 1 teaspoon salt
- 2 ounces (60g) semisweet chocolate, grated
- ¾ cup (180ml) whole milk
- 2 large eggs, room temperature,
  lightly beaten
- 1 tablespoon (15g) salted butter, softened
- 1 teaspoon instant coffee powder
- 1 teaspoon vanilla extract
- 2 ounces (60g) semisweet chocolate chips

For the ganache
- 8 ounces (225g) bittersweet chocolate, chopped
- 1 cup (240ml) heavy cream
- 1 teaspoon vanilla extract

METHOD

Preheat the oven to 325°F (160°F) and spray two 6-cup doughnut pans
with oil.

In a large bowl, whisk together the flour, sugar, cocoa powder, baking
powder, cinnamon, and salt. Add the grated chocolate and stir to blend.

In a separate bowl, whisk together the milk, eggs, softened butter, instant
coffee, and vanilla extract. Pour into the flour mixture, add the chocolate
chips, and stir to combine. Using a pastry bag (a disposable one or use a
plastic bag with the corner cut off), fill the doughnut pans three-quarters
full. Bake for about 10 minutes, or until a toothpick inserted in the center
comes out clean. Let cool in the pans for 5 minutes, then carefully transfer
the doughnuts to a wire rack to cool.

While the doughnuts are cooling, make the whipped topping. Place the
chocolate in a medium bowl. In a small pan, heat the heavy cream until it
just begins to simmer. Do not let it boil. Remove the cream from the heat
and pour it over the chocolate. Leave for 2 minutes, add the vanilla, and
whisk until the chocolate has melted and the mixture is smooth. Set aside
for an hour or two, until it has cooled, thickened, and set. Whip with an
electric mixer for 3–4 minutes, until it holds its shape. Pipe large swirls
onto the doughnuts before serving.

Makes 20

STRAWBERRY SHORTCAKE DOUGHNUTS

*Doughnuts make a great substitute for shortcake, and filled with whipped cream
and strawberries, these will be as popular as the originals.*

INGREDIENTS

For the doughnuts
- ½ cup (120ml) whole milk, warmed
- 1 teaspoon superfine sugar
- 1 envelope (2 ¼ teaspoons) active dry yeast
- 1 ¾ cups (220g) all-purpose flour, divided
- ½ teaspoon salt
- 1 large egg, room temperature, lightly beaten
- Zest of 1 lemon
- Vegetable oil for deep-frying

For the filling
- 2 cups (475ml) heavy cream
- ¼ cup (25g) powdered sugar, sifted
- About 16 strawberries, sliced

For the frosting
- ¾ cup (75g) powdered sugar, sifted
- 1 tablespoon whole milk
- 2 teaspoons smooth raspberry preserves

For the decoration
- Multicolored sugar strands

METHOD

Line two large cookie sheets with parchment paper.

Place the warm milk in a large bowl and stir in the sugar, yeast, and
½ cup (60g) flour. Leave for 10–15 minutes until frothy. Add the remaining
flour, salt, egg, and lemon zest, and mix until a soft dough comes together.
Turn out onto a lightly floured work surface, and knead, using your hands
and knuckles, for 10 minutes, until the dough is soft, smooth, and elastic.
Divide into 8 pieces and shape into balls, folding the edges of the dough
underneath and pinching together to seal well. Place balls on the cookie
sheets, about an inch (2.5cm) apart, with the seam underneath. Cover with
plastic wrap that has been sprayed with oil, and leave for about 30 minutes,
until slightly risen.

Heat the oil in a large pan until it reaches 360°F (182°C). Fry the doughnuts
for 2–3 minutes on each side, until golden brown, and drain on paper
towels. Cool on a wire rack. When cold, slice each doughnut in half
horizontally. Set aside the top halves.

Place the cream and powdered sugar in a large bowl, and whip together
until stiff peaks form. Arrange a layer of strawberries on the bottom halves
of the doughnuts, and divide the whipped cream between them.

Make the frosting. In a medium bowl, mix the powdered sugar with the
milk and raspberry preserves until smooth. Spread a little on the top
halves of the doughnuts, then place them on top of the whipped cream,
like a sandwich. Decorate the tops with a few multicolored sugar strands.
Serve immediately.

Makes 8

PRALINE PUMPKIN DOUGHNUTS

Pumpkins are for life, not just Thanksgiving, and are as tasty in doughnuts as they are in pies.

INGREDIENTS

For the frosting
- 6 ounces (170g) cream cheese, room temperature
- 1 ⅓ cups (130g) powdered sugar, sifted
- 1 teaspoon lemon juice

For the topping
- ⅓ cup (65g) superfine sugar
- 3 ounces (85g) whole unblanched almonds

For the doughnuts
- 2 cups (250g) all-purpose flour
- 1 ½ teaspoons baking powder
- 1 teaspoon ground cinnamon
- ½ teaspoon baking soda
- ½ teaspoon ground nutmeg
- ½ teaspoon ground ginger
- ½ teaspoon salt
- ¼ cup (60g) salted butter, melted
- ¼ cup (60g) Greek yogurt
- 1 ½ cups (370g) canned pumpkin purée (not pumpkin pie filling)
- 2 large eggs, room temperature
- 1 teaspoon vanilla extract
- 1 ½ cups (300g) superfine sugar
- ½ cup (60g) chopped pecans

For the decoration
- 2 tablespoons chopped pecans

METHOD

Preheat the oven to 350°F (175°C) and spray three 6-cup doughnut pans with oil. Smear a cookie sheet with vegetable oil.

Make the frosting. Beat the cream cheese, powdered sugar, and lemon juice until smooth. Chill for an hour before using.

Make the praline topping. In a small pan, heat the sugar and almonds gently, stirring occasionally, until the sugar caramelizes and the almonds begin to split. Turn onto the oiled cookie sheet and let cool. Crush in a food processor.

In a large bowl, whisk the flour, baking powder, ground cinnamon, baking soda, nutmeg, ginger, and salt together. In a separate bowl, whisk the melted butter, yogurt, and pumpkin purée together. Add the eggs and vanilla and mix well until combined. Add the sugar and chopped pecans and mix again. Add to the flour mixture and stir well. Using a disposable pastry bag, pipe the batter into the prepared doughnut cups, about two-thirds full. Bake for about 15 minutes, or until a toothpick inserted into the center comes out clean. Let cool in the pans for 5 minutes, then transfer to a wire rack to cool completely.

Spread the frosting around the tops of the doughnuts, and set back on the wire rack. For the decoration, mix 4 tablespoons crushed praline with 2 tablespoons chopped pecans, and sprinkle on top of the frosting before serving.

Makes 18

VEGAN PECAN PIE DOUGHNUTS

Not just for holidays, these richly flavored doughnuts can hold their own, and they're vegan!

INGREDIENTS

For the topping
- 1 cup (120g) whole pecans
- ¼ cup (50g) superfine sugar, or more if desired
- ½ tablespoon water
- ½ teaspoon ground cinnamon
- ¼ teaspoon salt
- ⅛ teaspoon vanilla extract

For the doughnuts
- 1 ¼ tablespoons cornstarch
- 1 ¼ tablespoons potato starch
- Heaping ¼ teaspoon baking powder
- ½ cup (60ml) water
- 1 teaspoon vegetable oil
- 2 tablespoons active dry yeast
- 1 cup (240ml) soy milk, warmed
- ½ cup (60g) white bread flour

- 3 cups (375g) all-purpose flour
- 1 teaspoon ground cinnamon
- ½ cup (60g) chopped toasted pecans
- ¼ cup (50g) vegetable shortening
- ½ tablespoon vanilla extract
- ¼ cup (50g) superfine sugar
- ½ teaspoon salt
- Vegetable oil for deep-frying

For the glaze
- 1 ½ tablespoons vegetable shortening
- 2 tablespoons brown sugar
- ½ tablespoon soy milk
- ½ teaspoon ground cinnamon
- Pinch salt
- ½ teaspoon vanilla extract

METHOD

Make pecan topping. Preheat oven to 250°F (120°C). Mix pecans with other topping ingredients to fully coat them. Spread on a cookie sheet. If you wish, roll pecans in extra sugar and cinnamon. Bake for 1 hour. Remove and cool, chop small, and set aside.

Whisk the cornstarch, potato starch, and baking powder. Whisk in water and oil until well combined. This is the egg replacer.

In a mixing bowl, dissolve yeast in milk. Add the bread flour and 1 ½ cups (190g) all-purpose flour, the cinnamon, and the chopped pecans. Mix in a stand mixer with paddle attachment until smooth. Cover and let rest for 20 minutes. Mix in shortening, then add vanilla and egg replacer. Turn off mixer, add sugar and salt, and then mix on low until dough starts to come together.

Using the dough hook, add remaining flour in three stages. The dough should pull away from the sides of the bowl, but still be sticky. If too sticky, add more flour; if too dry, add more milk. Cover and set in a warm place for 30 minutes. Gently press dough down and rest again for 1 hour, or until doubled. On a lightly floured surface, roll dough ½ inch (1.25cm) thick and cut with a 3 ½-inch (8.75cm) doughnut cutter. Place doughnuts on floured cookie sheets, cover with oiled plastic wrap, and let rest for 15–20 minutes. Heat oil in a heavy, large pan to 360°F (182°C). Fry doughnuts for 2 minutes per side, remove, and drain on paper towels.

Make the glaze. Combine all glaze ingredients in a pan over medium heat, stir, and bring to a boil. Remove from heat, stir, and allow to thicken, 3–5 minutes.

Dip doughnut tops in the glaze and place on paper towels. Before glaze is fully set, sprinkle with sugared pecans.

Makes about 12

MOIST CARROT CAKE DOUGHNUTS WITH CREAM CHEESE FROSTING

Very pretty, with coconut flakes and sweet frosting, these baked doughnuts are perfect for little girls, as they are an excellent blend of sugar and spice.

INGREDIENTS

For the frosting
- 4 ounces (115g) cream cheese, room temperature
- 1 cup (100g) powdered sugar, sifted
- 3 tablespoons (45g) salted butter, room temperature
- ½ teaspoon vanilla extract

For the doughnuts
- ½ cup (60g) all-purpose flour
- ¼ cup (30g) whole wheat flour
- ¼ cup (40g) rolled oats
- 1 teaspoon baking powder
- ½ teaspoon baking soda
- ¼ teaspoon salt
- 1 teaspoon ground cinnamon
- ½ teaspoon ground allspice
- ¼ teaspoon ground nutmeg
- ¼ cup (50g) brown sugar
- 1 large egg, room temperature, lightly beaten
- 3 tablespoons vegetable oil
- 2 tablespoons whole milk
- 1 teaspoon vanilla extract
- ¾ cup (50g) finely shredded carrots
- 2 tablespoons chopped walnuts

For the decoration
- ⅓ cup (50g) sweetened shredded coconut

METHOD

Preheat the oven to 350°F (175°C). Lightly spray a 6-cup doughnut pan with oil.

Make the frosting. In a medium bowl, beat the cream cheese, powdered sugar, butter, and vanilla with an electric whisk until smooth and no lumps remain. Cover and chill in the refrigerator for an hour before using.

In a large bowl, mix together the flours, oats, baking powder, baking soda, salt, cinnamon, allspice, nutmeg, and brown sugar. Make a well in the center and add the egg, milk, vegetable oil, and vanilla. Stir until just combined. Stir in the carrots and nuts. Spoon or pipe the mixture into the doughnut pan, and bake for 8–10 minutes, until a toothpick inserted into the center comes out clean. Let cool in the pan for 5 minutes, then transfer to a wire rack to cool completely.

Spread out the coconut on a cookie sheet and bake for 6–7 minutes, until lightly toasted, but not burned. Watch it carefully and stir once or twice during cooking.

Spread the frosting over the cooled doughnuts and decorate with the toasted coconut before serving.

Makes 6

GERMAN CHOCOLATE DOUGHNUTS

The pièce de résistance of these doughnuts is the frosting. Try not to eat the frosting before the doughnuts are finished!

INGREDIENTS

For the doughnuts
- 3 cups (375g) all-purpose flour
- 1 ⅛ cups (100g) unsweetened cocoa powder
- 2 cups (400g) superfine sugar
- 2 teaspoons baking soda
- Pinch salt
- ¾ cup (180ml) vegetable oil
- 2 cups (475ml) cold water
- 2 teaspoons vanilla extract
- 2 tablespoons white vinegar

For the frosting
- ⅓ cup (65g) superfine sugar
- 2 tablespoons (30g) unsalted butter
- 1 large egg, slightly beaten
- Scant ½ cup (120ml) evaporated milk
- ¾ cup (110g) shredded coconut
- ¼ cup (30g) chopped pecans
- 1 teaspoon vanilla extract

METHOD

Preheat oven to 350°F (175°C). With a nonstick spray, spray two 12-cup doughnut pans.

In the bowl of a stand mixer, combine the flour, cocoa, sugar, baking soda, and salt. On low speed, slowly add the oil, water, vanilla, and vinegar. Mix until smooth. The batter will be thin.

Fill the doughnut cups three-quarters full with batter. Bake for 10–12 minutes, or until a toothpick inserted in the center of a doughnut comes out clean. Let the doughnuts cool in the pans for 5 minutes, then carefully transfer to cooling racks to finish cooling.

Make the frosting. In a medium saucepan over medium heat, combine the sugar, butter, egg, and evaporated milk. Whisk while cooking, making sure the frosting does not stick to the pan. Continue cooking until the mixture becomes thick, about 10 minutes. Remove from the heat and let rest for 5 minutes. Stir in the coconut, pecans, and vanilla, and continue stirring for 3 minutes.

Spread the tops of the cooled doughnuts with an ample amount of frosting before serving.

Makes 24

BANANA CREAM PIE DOUGHNUTS

Why should pies have all the fun? From the softness of the doughnut to the creaminess of the banana, these doughnuts have all that their namesake pie does, and more!

INGREDIENTS

For the filling
- 1 large ripe banana, sliced
- 2 tablespoons (30g) unsalted butter
- 2 tablespoons brown sugar
- 2 cups (475ml) whole milk
- ⅓ cup (65g) superfine sugar
- 3 tablespoons cornstarch
- 1 large egg
- 1 teaspoon vanilla extract

For the doughnuts
- 2 tablespoons active dry yeast
- 1 cup (240ml) whole milk, warmed
- ½ cup (60g) white bread flour
- 3 cups (375g) all-purpose flour
- ¼ cup (60g) cold unsalted butter, grated
- 1 teaspoon vanilla extract
- 2 large eggs
- 1 large egg yolk

- 2 tablespoons plain yogurt
- ¼ cup (50g) superfine sugar
- ½ teaspoon salt
- Vegetable oil for deep-frying

For the topping
- ¼ cup (60ml) heavy cream
- 1 teaspoon powdered sugar, or to taste
- Vanilla extract, to taste

For the decoration
- 1 slightly firm small banana, chopped (optional)
- ½ cup (50g) crushed vanilla wafers

METHOD

Make the filling. Sauté bananas for 1 minute in butter and brown sugar. Remove and mash. Over medium heat, whisk milk, sugar, and cornstarch. Just before it boils, whisk in mashed bananas until smooth. Beat eggs and slowly stir in a little hot banana mixture. Then add eggs to the pan and let boil for 2 minutes, or until thick. Remove from heat, stir in vanilla, cool slightly, put plastic wrap directly on top of filling, and chill.

In mixing bowl, dissolve yeast in milk. Add bread flour and 1 ½ cups (190g) all-purpose flour. Mix in a stand mixer with paddle attachment until smooth. Cover and rest for 20 minutes. Gradually add butter and mix well. Add vanilla, eggs, egg yolk, and yogurt. Turn off mixer, add sugar and salt, then mix on low until dough starts to come together.

With the dough hook, add remaining flour in three stages. The dough should pull away from the sides of the bowl, but still be slightly sticky. If too wet, add a little more flour. Cover, set in a warm place for 30 minutes, then punch down and leave for 1 hour, or until doubled.

On a lightly floured surface, roll dough ½ inch (1.25cm) thick. Cut rounds with a 3 ½-inch (8.75cm) biscuit cutter, place on floured cookie sheets, cover with oiled plastic wrap, and let rise for 15 minutes.

Heat oil in a large, heavy pan to 360°F (182°C). Fry doughnuts for 3 minutes on the first side, 2 minutes on the second side, remove, and drain and cool on paper towels. When cooled, cut almost in half, spread with filling, add a few chopped bananas if desired, and replace the top.

Make the topping. Beat cream, sugar, and vanilla until stiff peaks form. To serve, top doughnut with whipped cream and crushed vanilla wafers.

Makes about 12

ROCKY ROAD DOUGHNUTS

This doughnut hits the mother lode! Chocolate, nuts, and marshmallow come together to create the perfect doughnut.

INGREDIENTS

For the doughnuts
- ¼ cup (50g) superfine sugar
- 1 large egg
- 1 tablespoon active dry yeast
- 1 cup (240ml) whole milk, warmed
- ½ tablespoon vanilla extract
- ⅔ cup (60g) unsweetened cocoa powder
- 1 teaspoon salt
- 1 teaspoon baking soda
- ½ cup (60g) chopped walnuts
- 3 cups (375g) all-purpose flour
- ½ cup (115g) cold unsalted butter, grated

For the glaze
- ¾ cup (75g) powdered sugar, sifted
- 2 tablespoons heavy cream
- 2 tablespoons (30g) unsalted butter, cubed
- 1 ¼ cups (100g) mini marshmallows

For the decoration
- ¾ cup (100g) chopped toasted walnuts
- Chocolate shavings (optional)

METHOD

In the bowl of a stand mixer with the paddle attachment, beat sugar and egg until blended. Add the yeast, milk, vanilla, cocoa powder, salt, baking soda, and walnuts. Stir to blend. With the mixer on low, add 2 cups (250g) flour, ½ cup (60g) at a time, until the dough pulls away from the sides of the bowl.

Switching to the dough hook, slowly add the butter until fully incorporated. On low speed, add the remaining flour. The dough should now be soft, but not too sticky. Knead the dough gently on a lightly floured surface until it is no longer sticky. Butter the inside of a bowl and place the dough ball inside. Cover with plastic wrap and allow the dough to double in size, about 45 minutes.

Preheat oven to 375°F (190°C) and place parchment on large cookie sheets. Gently press dough down with your fist and roll out ½ inch (1.25cm) thick. Cut out doughnuts with a 3 ½-inch (8.75cm) doughnut cutter and set an inch (2.5cm) apart on the cookie sheets. Cover with oiled plastic wrap and let rise until doubled, about 15 minutes. Bake for 10–12 minutes or until doughnuts spring back at the touch. Let cool on pans for 1 minute, then transfer to cooling racks.

Make the marshmallow glaze. In a medium pan, whisk together powdered sugar and heavy cream. Place pan over medium-low heat, whisking continually. After 1 minute, add the butter. Once the butter has melted, slowly add the marshmallows while stirring constantly with a wooden spoon until you reach the desired consistency. Working quickly, dip the tops of the cooled doughnuts in the marshmallow glaze and place on paper towels. While the glaze is still warm, sprinkle with chopped nuts. For extra chocolate, you may also sprinkle chocolate shavings on top.

Makes about 12

CHOCOLATE MACAROON DOUGHNUTS

The addictive blend of chocolate and coconut just got better. With these ingredients sitting atop a chewy doughnut, nothing could be better!

INGREDIENTS

For the doughnuts
- 2 tablespoons active dry yeast
- ¾ cup (180ml) whole milk, warmed
- ¼ cup (60ml) coconut milk, warmed
- ½ cup (60g) white bread flour
- 2 ½ cups (315g) all-purpose flour
- ½ cup (45g) unsweetened cocoa powder
- ¼ cup (60g) cold unsalted butter, grated
- 1 teaspoon vanilla extract
- 2 large eggs
- 1 large egg yolk
- 2 tablespoons plain yogurt
- ½ cup (70g) toasted coconut
- ¼ cup (50g) superfine sugar
- 1 teaspoon salt
- Vegetable oil for deep-frying

For the glaze
- ¼ cup (60ml) heavy cream
- 3 tablespoons (45g) cold unsalted butter, grated
- ⅙ cup (40ml) light corn syrup
- 3 ounces (85g) bittersweet chocolate, coarsely chopped
- ½ teaspoon vanilla extract

For the decoration
- ½ cup (70g) toasted coconut

METHOD

In a large bowl, dissolve yeast in the milks. Add the bread flour, 1 ½ cups (190g) all-purpose flour, and the cocoa powder. Mix in a stand mixer with the paddle attachment until smooth. Cover and let rest for 20 minutes. Slowly add the butter and mix until combined. Then add the vanilla extract, eggs, egg yolk, yogurt, and toasted coconut. Turn off mixer and add the sugar and salt. Mix on low until the dough starts to come together.

Switching to the dough hook attachment, add the remaining all-purpose flour in three stages. The dough should pull away from the sides of the bowl nicely, but still be sticky. Cover and set in a warm place for 30 minutes. Gently press dough down with your fist and let rest again for 1 hour, or until dough has doubled in size.

On a lightly floured surface, roll dough ½ inch (1.25cm) thick. Cut rounds with a 3 ½-inch (8.75cm) doughnut cutter, place on floured cookie sheets, cover with oiled plastic wrap, and let rise for 15 minutes.

Heat oil in a large, heavy pan to 360°F (182°C). Fry a few doughnuts at a time for 2 minutes per side, remove, and drain on paper towels. Let cool.

Make the chocolate glaze. In a medium saucepan over low heat, mix the cream, butter, and corn syrup, stirring continuously with a wooden spoon. After 2 minutes, add the chocolate and continue to stir. When the mixture reaches the desired consistency, take pan off heat, stir in the vanilla, and stir for 1 minute more. Dip the tops of the doughnuts in the warm glaze and place on paper towels to set. While the glaze is still warm, sprinkle with toasted coconut.

Makes about 12

Chapter 8

ONLY SLIGHTLY SAVORY

Sugary sweetness not your thing? How about starting your day with a Spicy
Savory Plantain Breakfast Doughnut Sandwich, or a Maple and Bacon Bar?
Adding cheese, figs, ham, or pretzels to an already perfect creation (the
doughnut), makes endless possibilities
for amazingness!

SAFFRON DOUGHNUTS WITH LEMON YOGURT FILLING

These doughnuts, delicately spiced with saffron, are filled with an exotic and creamy lemon yogurt, flavored with nutmeg, cardamom, and pistachio nuts.

INGREDIENTS

For the filling
- 1 cup (240ml) good-quality lemon yogurt
- 1 cup (100g) powdered sugar, sifted
- ¼ teaspoon crushed cardamom seeds
- Pinch saffron
- ¼ teaspoon ground nutmeg
- 1 tablespoon finely crushed shelled pistachio nuts
- 1 cup (200g) superfine sugar
- 1 cup (240ml) heavy cream

For the doughnuts
- ¾ cup (180ml) plus 2 tablespoons whole milk, warmed
- 1 teaspoon superfine sugar
- 1 package (2 ¼ teaspoons) active dry yeast
- 2 ¾ cups (350g) self-rising flour
- ¾ cup (90g) white bread flour
- ⅓ cup (65g) superfine sugar
- ½ teaspoon salt
- ¼ cup (60g) salted butter, melted and cooled slightly
- 2 tablespoons lemon yogurt
- Zest of 1 lemon
- ¼ teaspoon saffron
- Vegetable oil for deep-frying

METHOD

Make the base for the filling one or two days before. Place the yogurt in cheesecloth or clean muslin cloth and tie it tightly with string to form a bag. Suspend bag over a large bowl, and leave for 24–48 hours while the water drips away. When the yogurt has thickened, put it in a bowl, add the powdered sugar, and stir briskly with a wooden spoon until smooth and all the lumps are gone. Add the crushed cardamom, saffron, nutmeg, and pistachio nuts. Cover and refrigerate until needed.

Place the warm milk in a medium bowl, stir in the teaspoon of sugar and the yeast, and leave for 10–15 minutes.

Line two large cookie sheets with parchment paper.

With the dough hook in the bowl of a stand mixer, stir both the flours, ⅓ cup (65g) superfine sugar, and salt. Add the yeast liquid, butter, lemon yogurt, and lemon zest, and mix until the dough comes together. On medium speed, mix for 2 minutes. The dough should be slightly sticky. If too wet, add more flour; too dry, add more water. Wait 2 minutes, add the saffron, and mix for 2 minutes. Transfer the dough to a lightly oiled bowl, cover, and leave for an hour.

On a lightly floured work surface, punch down the dough and knead twice. Divide it into 15 equal pieces and roll into balls, pinching to seal. Place the balls one inch (2.5cm) apart on the cookie sheets, seam underneath. Cover with oiled plastic wrap and leave for an hour.

Heat the oil in a heavy, large pan to 360°F (182°C). Fry the doughnuts for 3 minutes on the first side, 2 minutes on the second side. Drain on paper towels, roll in 1 cup (200g) superfine sugar, and cool on a wire rack.

Split each doughnut almost in half horizontally. To finish the filling, whip the heavy cream with the superfine sugar until it holds its shape, and gently fold in the spiced lemon yogurt mixture. Pipe decoratively into each doughnut. Serve immediately.

Makes 15

SPICY SAVORY PLANTAIN BREAKFAST DOUGHNUT SANDWICH

Plantains are very versatile and their flavor blends beautifully with cheese.
Throw in a few crushed chili flakes for a surprising kick.

INGREDIENTS

- 7 Simple Glazed Ring Doughnuts (page 65)

For the filling
- ⅓ cup (75g) salted butter, room temperature, for spreading
- 1 tablespoon vegetable oil
- 2 ripe plantains, peeled and cut into ¼-inch- (6mm-) thick slices
- Pinch salt
- 7 slices cheddar cheese
- Crushed chili flakes (optional)

METHOD

Prepare the recipe for Simple Glazed Ring Doughnuts.

Carefully split each doughnut in half horizontally. Spread each cut half with butter. In a large skillet, heat 1 tablespoon oil, add the plantains, and fry in batches for a minute on each side, until nicely browned. Drain on paper towels.

Add a little more oil to the pan. Place the doughnut halves, buttered side down, in the frying pan. Sprinkle the doughnut halves with a little salt. Place cheese and a few plantain slices on half of the doughnut halves.

If you are a chili lover, sprinkle on a few crushed chili flakes. Allow the doughnuts to brown a bit and get warm, and top the filled side with the other doughnut half. Press down gently with a spatula and continue cooking until the cheese melts a little. Transfer to a serving plate. Serve immediately.

Makes 7 doughnut sandwiches

TIP
The key to perfect fried plantains is to ensure that they are at the right degree of ripeness. The riper they are, the sweeter. The skin should be almost black, or in some cases, have a dull yellow color with patches of black. They should peel easily and cook quickly.

MAPLE AND BACON BARS WITH MAPLE VANILLA GLAZE AND BACON BITS

Doughnut bars are sometimes called Long Johns. Crumbling the crispy bacon on top of the maple frosting means you get the full flavor of both in every delicious bite.

INGREDIENTS

For the doughnuts
- ¼ cup (60ml) warm water
- 1 teaspoon superfine sugar
- 2 packages (4 ½ teaspoons) active dried yeast
- 1 ⅓ cups (315ml) whole milk, warmed
- ½ cup (100g) superfine sugar
- ⅓ cup (70g) shortening
- 1 teaspoon salt
- 2 large eggs, room temperature, lightly beaten
- 1 tablespoon maple syrup
- 4 ¼ cups (500g) all-purpose flour
- Vegetable oil for deep-frying

For the topping
- 1 pound (450g) hickory-smoked bacon, cooked until very crispy, and chopped

For the glaze
- 2 tablespoons dark corn syrup
- 2 tablespoons maple syrup
- 2 ½ cups (250g) powdered sugar, sifted
- 1 teaspoon maple extract
- Pinch salt

METHOD

Place the warm water in a small bowl, stir in the teaspoon of sugar and the yeast, and leave for 10–15 minutes.

With the dough hook in the bowl of a stand mixer, mix together the yeast liquid, warm milk, sugar, shortening, salt, eggs, maple syrup, and 2 cups (250g) flour. Mix for 3 minutes on low speed. Add the remaining flour, ½ cup (60g) at a time, until a dough comes together and no longer sticks to the side of the bowl. The dough should be slightly sticky. If too wet, add more flour; too dry, add more water. Cover and leave for an hour.

Transfer to a lightly floured work surface and punch down. Roll out to a 8 x 9-inch (20 x 23cm) rectangle, ¼ inch (6mm) thick. Cut into 12 bars, each one about 1 ½ x 4 inches (0.6 x 10cm) in size. Spread the bars out slightly, so that they are no longer touching, cover them with oiled plastic wrap, and leave for 30 minutes.

Heat the oil in a large pan to 360°F (182°C). Carefully slide the bars into the hot oil, risen side first. Cook for 1 minute; flip them over and cook for 1 minute; flip again and cook 1 more minute (a total of 3 minutes). Drain on paper towels, then transfer to a wire rack to cool slightly.

Place the bacon pieces on a large plate.

Make the glaze. Warm the corn syrup and maple syrup gently in a small pan. Add the sugar ½ cup (100g) at a time, stirring briskly with a wooden spoon until the glaze is smooth and a slightly runny consistency, perfect for dipping. Remove from the heat and stir in the maple extract and salt. Dip the tops of the doughnut bars into the glaze, then press them onto the bacon pieces. Serve immediately.

Makes 12

CHOCOLATE PEANUT BUTTER PRETZEL DOUGHNUTS

These sweet and salty baked doughnuts are smothered in a rich chocolate frosting, topped with broken pretzels, and drizzled with white chocolate.

INGREDIENTS

For the doughnuts
- 2 tablespoons warm water
- 1 teaspoon superfine sugar
- 1 package (2 ¼ teaspoons) instant yeast
- 2 cups (250g) all-purpose flour
- 1 ¼ cups (250g) superfine sugar
- 1 ½ teaspoons baking powder
- ½ teaspoon ground nutmeg
- ½ teaspoon salt
- 2 large eggs, room temperature
- 1 cup (240ml) vanilla yogurt
- ¼ cup (60g) unsalted butter, melted
- 2 teaspoons vanilla extract

For the vanilla glaze
- ¼ cup (60g) unsalted butter
- 1 ½ cups (150g) powdered sugar, sifted
- 2 teaspoons vanilla extract
- 3 tablespoons evaporated milk

For the chocolate glaze
- 4 ounces (115g) semisweet chocolate, roughly chopped
- 2 tablespoons (30g) unsalted butter
- 1 tablespoon smooth peanut butter
- 1 cup (100g) powdered sugar, sifted
- 1 teaspoon vanilla extract
- 4 tablespoons evaporated milk

For the decoration
- 1 cup (100g) small pretzels, roughly broken
- 2 ounces (60g) white chocolate, melted

METHOD

Preheat the oven to 350°F (175°C) and spray two 6-cup doughnut pans with oil. Line two large cookie sheets with parchment paper.

Place the warm water in a small bowl, stir in the teaspoon of sugar and the yeast, and leave for 10–15 minutes. In a medium bowl, whisk together flour, sugar, baking powder, nutmeg, and salt.

In another bowl, whisk the eggs, yogurt, melted butter, and vanilla. Pour into the dry ingredients with the yeast liquid. Stir until combined. Transfer the batter to a disposable pastry bag and pipe into the prepared pans, filling each cup about two-thirds full. Some mixture will be left, so wash and dry one pan after baking and repeat with the remaining mixture.

Bake the doughnuts for 15 minutes. Remove from the oven, let cool in the pan for 5 minutes, and cool on a wire rack.

Make the vanilla glaze. Gently warm the butter until melted. Add the powdered sugar, vanilla, and evaporated milk, and stir briskly with a wooden spoon until smooth. Add a little more milk if needed. Remove from heat.

Dip half of each doughnut in the vanilla glaze, flip over, and dip the other half. Place on the cookie sheets to set, about 30 minutes. After 15 minutes, flip them over to set the underside.

Make the chocolate glaze. Gently warm the chocolate and butter until melted. Add the peanut butter, powdered sugar, vanilla, and milk, and stir briskly with a wooden spoon until smooth. Add a little more milk if needed. Remove from heat.

Dip the top of each doughnut in the chocolate glaze and place on a wire rack. Cover with broken pretzels and drizzle with a little melted white chocolate. Let set before serving.

Makes 16

FRIED SMOKED HAM BREAKFAST DOUGHNUT SANDWICH

Thrill your friends and family with your inventiveness with a doughnut breakfast sandwich,
filled with ham, egg, and cheese, with a dollop of ketchup in the hole.

INGREDIENTS

- 7 Simple Glazed Ring Doughnuts (page 65)

For the filling
- ⅓ cup (75g) salted butter, room temperature, for spreading
- 1 tablespoon vegetable oil
- Pinch salt
- 7 thin slices smoked ham
- 7 fried eggs
- 7 slices cheddar cheese
- ⅓ cup (80ml) ketchup
- Vegetable oil for deep-frying

METHOD

Prepare the recipe for Simple Glazed Ring Doughnuts.

Carefully split each doughnut in half horizontally, and spread each cut half with butter. In a large skillet, heat 1 tablespoon oil. Place the doughnut halves, buttered side down, in the frying pan. Sprinkle the doughnut halves with a little salt, and place a slice of ham, one fried egg, and a slice of cheese on half of the doughnut halves.

Fry the doughnuts until browned and warm, and top the filled side with the other half of the doughnut. Press down gently with a spatula, and continue cooking until the cheese melts a little. Transfer to a serving plate, and squirt a dollop of ketchup into the hole on the top of each doughnut sandwich. Serve immediately.

Makes 7 doughnut sandwiches

SWEET POTATO AND MAPLE DOUGHNUTS

Need a break from the usual pumpkin desserts? Sweet potato and maple form an alliance that won't make you feel guilty.

INGREDIENTS

For the doughnuts
- 3 ½ cups (440g) all-purpose flour
- 4 teaspoons baking powder
- ½ teaspoon baking soda
- 1 teaspoon salt
- 2 teaspoons ground cinnamon
- ½ teaspoon ground ginger
- ¼ teaspoon ground nutmeg
- ⅛ teaspoon ground cloves
- 3 tablespoons (45g) cold unsalted butter, grated
- 1 cup (200g) superfine sugar
- 1 large egg
- 2 large egg yolks
- 1 teaspoon vanilla extract
- ½ cup (120ml) plus 1 tablespoon buttermilk
- 1 cup (250g) canned pumpkin purée (not pumpkin pie filling)
- 1 cup (250g) cooked mashed sweet potato
- Vegetable oil for deep-frying

For the glaze
- 2 cups (200g) powdered sugar, sifted
- 4 tablespoons heavy cream
- 2 tablespoons maple syrup
- 1 teaspoon maple extract

METHOD

Whisk the flour, baking powder, baking soda, salt, and spices in a medium bowl to blend.

In the bowl of a stand mixer, cream the butter and sugar until blended. Beat in the egg, then the egg yolks and vanilla. Gradually beat in the buttermilk. Beat in the mashed sweet potato in four additions. Using a rubber spatula, fold in the dry ingredients in four additions, blending gently after each addition. Cover the bowl with plastic wrap and chill for 3 hours.

Remove the dough from the refrigerator and roll out ½ inch (1.25cm) thick. Cut dough with a 3 ½-inch (8.75cm) doughnut cutter. Place on floured cookie sheets, cover with oiled plastic wrap, and put back in refrigerator for 20 minutes.

Heat the oil in a large, heavy pan to 360°F (182°C). Gently place a few doughnuts in the pan at a time. Fry for 2 minutes per side, then remove with a slotted spoon and place on paper towels to drain and cool while making the glaze.

Make the glaze. In a medium bowl, whisk all the ingredients together until the desired consistency. Dip the tops of the doughnuts in the glaze and place on paper towels to set.

Makes about 24

CARDAMOM DOUGHNUTS WITH APPLE CIDER GLAZE

Spicy cardamom and tangy apple cider team up and the results are awesome.

INGREDIENTS

For the doughnuts
- 2 tablespoons active dry yeast
- 1 cup (240ml) whole milk, warmed
- ½ cup (60g) white bread flour
- 3 cups (375g) all-purpose flour
- ¼ cup (60g) cold unsalted butter, grated
- 1 teaspoon vanilla extract
- 2 large eggs
- 1 egg yolk
- 2 tablespoons plain yogurt
- 2 tablespoons superfine sugar
- ½ teaspoon salt
- Pinch ground cardamom
- Vegetable oil for deep-frying

For the glaze
- 1 cup (100g) powdered sugar, sifted
- 2 ½ tablespoons apple cider
- ½ tablespoon heavy cream
- ½ teaspoon vanilla extract

METHOD

In a large mixing bowl, dissolve yeast in milk. Add the bread flour and 1 ½ cups (190g) all-purpose flour. Mix in a stand mixer with the paddle attachment until smooth. Cover and let rest for 20 minutes. Gradually add the butter and mix until incorporated. Add the vanilla, eggs, egg yolk, and yogurt. Turn off mixer; add the sugar, salt, and cardamom; then mix on low until the dough starts to come together.

With the dough hook attachment, add the remaining all-purpose flour in three stages. The dough should pull away from the sides of the bowl nicely, but still be slightly sticky. If too wet, add a little more flour. Cover and set in a warm place for 30 minutes. Gently press the dough down with your fist and let sit again for 1 hour, or until the dough has doubled.

Turn dough out onto a lightly floured surface and roll ½ inch (1.25cm) thick. Cut rounds using a 3 ½-inch (8.75cm) doughnut cutter, place on floured cookie sheets, cover with oiled plastic wrap, and let rise for 15 minutes.

Heat the oil in a large, heavy pan to 360°F (182°C). Gently place a few doughnuts in the pan at a time. Fry for 2 minutes on each side, then remove with a slotted spoon and place on paper towels.

Make the glaze. In a small bowl, whisk together the powdered sugar, apple cider, and heavy cream to desired consistency. Dip the tops of the doughnuts in the glaze and place on paper towels to set.

Makes about 12

CHEESE FRITTERS

Need an easy but tasty appetizer for a party? These richly flavored fritters are perfect for a football game or a cocktail party.

INGREDIENTS

For the fritters
- 4 large eggs, lightly beaten
- 1 cup (125g) all-purpose flour
- 2 ½ cups (270g) bread crumbs (Panko work best)
- 2 cups (200g) grated sharp cheddar cheese
- 2 cups (500g) ricotta cheese
- ½ teaspoon salt
- ½ teaspoon ground black pepper
- Crushed red chili flakes (optional)

For the dipping sauce (optional)
- 1 cup (240ml) ketchup
- ¼ teaspoon ground cayenne pepper

METHOD

Place the beaten eggs, flour, and bread crumbs in three separate bowls.

In a large bowl, combine the cheddar and ricotta cheese with the seasonings. Scoop tablespoon-sized balls of cheese mixture; roll in the flour, then in the eggs, then in the bread crumbs; and place on a cookie sheet. Press into ½-inch- (1.25cm-) thick patties.

Heat the oil in a heavy, large pan to 360°F (182°C). Fry the fritters, a few at a time, for 1 ½ minutes on each side, then remove with a slotted spoon and place on paper towels to drain.

Make the dipping sauce, if using. In a small serving bowl, mix together ketchup and cayenne pepper. Serve with the hot cheese fritters as a dipping sauce.

Makes about 16

PARSNIP DOUGHNUTS WITH PEAR AND HONEY GLAZE

Never tried parsnips before? Well, introduce yourself to this surprising combination with just a hint of sweet.

INGREDIENTS

For the doughnuts
- 3 ½ cups (440g) all-purpose flour
- 4 teaspoons baking powder
- 1 teaspoon salt
- ½ teaspoon baking soda
- ⅛ teaspoon ground nutmeg
- 3 tablespoons (45g) cold unsalted butter, grated
- 1 cup (200g) superfine sugar
- 1 large egg
- 2 large egg yolks
- 1 teaspoon vanilla extract
- ½ cup (120ml) plus 1 tablespoon buttermilk
- 1 ½ cups (375g) cooked, mashed parsnips (about 4–5 big parsnips)

For the topping
- 3 large firm, ripe pears (Bosc work best), cored and sliced into 8
- 1 cup (240ml) dry white wine
- 1 tablespoon superfine sugar
- ½ teaspoon ground cinnamon

For the glaze
- 1 cup (240ml) honey
- 2 tablespoons light corn syrup
- ¼ teaspoon ground cinnamon

For the decoration (optional)
- Ground nutmeg

METHOD

Whisk flour, baking powder, salt, baking soda, and nutmeg in a medium bowl to blend.

In the bowl of a stand mixer, cream the butter and sugar until blended. Beat in the egg, then the egg yolks and vanilla. Gradually beat in the buttermilk. Beat in the mashed parsnip in four additions. Using a rubber spatula, fold in the dry ingredients in four additions, blending gently after each addition. Cover with plastic wrap and chill for 3 hours.

Make the pear topping. In a medium saucepan, place pears, wine, sugar, and cinnamon. Simmer over medium-low heat for 20 minutes. Remove from heat and let cool.

Remove dough from refrigerator and roll out to ½-inch (1.25cm) thickness. Cut dough using a 3 ½-inch (8.75cm) doughnut cutter. Place doughnuts an inch (2.5cm) apart on floured cookie sheets, cover with oiled plastic wrap, and put back in the refrigerator for 20 minutes.

Heat the oil in a large, heavy pan to 360°F (182°C). Fry for 2 minutes on each side, remove with a slotted spoon, and place on paper towels. Allow to cool while making the glaze.

Make the glaze. Whisk together the glaze ingredients to desired consistency. Dip tops of doughnuts in the glaze and place on paper towels. While the glaze is still warm, fan out pears on top of each doughnut. Sprinkle with a tiny bit of nutmeg to finish, if desired.

Makes about 24

PARMESAN AND HONEY DOUGHNUTS

Fancy? Yes. Hard? No. With just a few simple ingredients added to the standard doughnut recipe,
you can create a lightly sweet and savory doughnut to please just about anyone.

INGREDIENTS

For the doughnuts
- 2 tablespoons active dry yeast
- 1 cup (240ml) whole milk, warmed
- ½ cup (60g) white bread flour
- 2 ½ cups (250g) all-purpose flour
- ¼ cup (60g) cold unsalted butter, grated
- 2 large eggs
- 1 large egg yolk
- 2 tablespoons plain yogurt
- ¼ cup (50g) superfine sugar
- ½ cup (50g) freshly grated
  Parmesan cheese
- ½ teaspoon salt
- Vegetable oil for deep-frying

For the glaze
- ½ cup (120ml) honey
- 1 tablespoon light corn syrup

For the decoration (optional)
- Freshly grated Parmesan cheese

METHOD

In a large mixing bowl, dissolve yeast in milk. Add the bread flour and 1 ½ cups (190g) all-purpose flour. Mix in a stand mixer with the paddle attachment until smooth. Cover and let rest for 20 minutes. Gradually add the butter and mix until incorporated. Add the eggs, egg yolk, and yogurt. Turn off mixer; add the sugar, cheese, and salt; then mix on low until the dough starts to come together.

With the dough hook attachment, add the remaining all-purpose flour in three stages. The dough should pull away from the sides of the bowl nicely, but still be sticky. Cover and set in a warm place for 30 minutes. Gently press the dough down with your fist and let sit again for 1 hour, or until the dough has doubled.

Turn dough out onto a lightly floured surface and roll ½ inch (1.25cm) thick. Cut rounds using a 3 ½-inch (8.75cm) doughnut cutter, place an inch (2.5cm) apart on floured cookie sheets, cover with oiled plastic wrap, and let rise for 15 minutes. Heat the oil in a large, heavy pan to 360°F (182°C). Gently place a few doughnuts in the pan at a time. Fry for 2 minutes per side, remove with a slotted spoon, and place on paper towels.

Make the glaze. Over medium-low heat, combine honey and corn syrup. Stir with a wooden spoon until the mixture thins a little, about 3 minutes. Dip the tops of the doughnuts in the glaze and place on paper towels. If you wish, sprinkle the tops with extra Parmesan for a finished look.

Makes about 12

OLIVE, CHOPPED FIGS, AND BRIE DOUGHNUT

The ultimate "wow factor" doughnut. These look and taste way more extravagant than they are to make. Paired with champagne and a sparkly dress, you can't go wrong!

INGREDIENTS

For the doughnuts
- ¼ cup (50g) superfine sugar
- 1 large egg
- 1 tablespoon active dry yeast
- 1 cup (240ml) whole milk, warmed
- 1 teaspoon salt
- 3 cups (375g) all-purpose flour
- ½ cup (115g) cold unsalted butter, grated
- 1 cup (120g) chopped green olives

For the topping
- 6 ounces (170g) Brie
- ¾ cup (90g) chopped dried figs
  (Black Mission figs work best)

METHOD

In the bowl of a stand mixer with the paddle attachment, beat sugar and egg until blended. Add the yeast, milk, and salt. Stir to blend. Add 2 cups (250g) flour, ½ cup (60g) at a time. With the mixer on low, mix until the dough pulls from the sides of the bowl.

Switching to the dough hook, slowly add the butter until fully incorporated. On low speed, add the remaining flour. Add the chopped olives and mix for 10 seconds. The dough should now be soft, but not too sticky.

Knead the dough gently on a lightly floured surface until it is no longer sticky. Butter the inside of a large bowl and place the dough ball inside. Cover with plastic wrap, set in a warm place, and let the dough double in size, about 45 minutes.

Preheat oven to 375°F (190°C). Cover large cookie sheets with parchment paper. Gently press dough down with your fist and roll out to ½-inch (1.25cm) thickness. Cut out doughnuts with a 3 ½-inch (8.75cm) doughnut cutter. Set doughnuts an inch (2.5cm) part on the cookie sheets. Cover with oiled plastic wrap and allow to rise until doubled in size, about 15 minutes.

Bake doughnuts until they are a light brown, approximately 10–12 minutes. Be careful not to overbake. Remove doughnuts from the oven. Slice small sections of Brie and place on top of each doughnut. Return doughnuts to the oven just until the cheese is slightly melted.

Remove doughnuts from the oven and sprinkle the tops with chopped figs. Serve warm.

Makes about 12

INDEX

ACKNOWLEDGMENTS

We would like to thank all our eager friends, neighbors, and family members (aka taste testers) whose comments and accolades helped to perfect these recipes. The wonderful team at Quintet deserve a special mention for organizing and supporting us through the writing process. And finally, we would like to thank each other—for the wealth of new and improved techniques, baking expertise, and pure dough-spiration that we've shared between our doughnut-loving continents.